OUTLIVE
DIET RECIPES

THE ULTIMATE OUTLIVE PLAN COOKBOOK

OVER 65 DELECTABLE RECIPES
FOR A HEALTHIER, LONGER LIFE

DYLAN GIOVAN

For permissions contact: werise.publish@gmail.com

Outlive Diet Recipes, First Edition

ISBN: 979-8851947803

Written by: Dylan Giovan

Typesetting and text makeup by: We Rise Publishing

Image rights: Ella Olsson/Unsplash

Printed in the United States of America

MAKE THE CHANGE,
NOT ONLY FOR YOURSELF

We are excited to introduce you to the "Outlive Diet Recipes", a culinary journey designed to help you embrace a healthier and more fulfilling lifestyle. But it's more than just a cookbook. It's an opportunity for you to make a difference in the lives of those less fortunate.

With every purchase of this workbook, we are committed to donating some of the proceeds to support a noble cause: feeding the less fortunate, particularly in third-world countries. We believe that food is a basic human right and that everyone should have access to nutritious meals.

By choosing to embark on this culinary adventure, you're not only making positive changes for yourself, but you're also making a meaningful impact in the lives of others. The donations generated from your purchase will go towards initiatives to alleviate hunger and provide sustenance to those who need it most.

This book represents the importance of food, not just as a means of nourishment, but as a catalyst for positive change. Through these recipes and the act of cooking, we hope to inspire a sense of gratitude for the abundance we enjoy and a desire to extend that abundance to those who are less fortunate.

YOUR FREE GIFT

I wanted to take a moment to express our gratitude for your recent purchase from us. As a token of our appreciation, we did a partnership with "PeakRead Publishing" to offer you their workbook for the book "OUTLIVE by Peter Attia" for free!

To claim your free workbook, simply scan the QR code below with your smartphone or tablet, and follow the download instructions.

In addition to the GIFT, you'll also have access to exclusive giveaways, discounts, and other valuable information.

TABLE OF CONTENTS

INTRODUCTION

We extend our sincerest appreciation to you for choosing to invest your valuable time and energy in acquiring and perusing this book. Your decision to embark on a journey towards a healthier and more fulfilling lifestyle is commendable, and we are thrilled to be your companions along this transformative path. Within the pages that follow, we invite you to uncover a hidden secret—a revelation centered around the utilization of nutritious recipes designed to enhance your cognitive abilities, maintain a fit physique, and unlock the potential for a longer, more vibrant life. By optimizing your gut health, nurturing your brain power, shedding excess weight, and defying the effects of aging, "Outlive Diet Recipes" holds the key to not only cheating the hands of time but also reveling in a decade-younger existence.

In today's fast-paced society, time is an invaluable commodity that we all cherish. We find ourselves constantly hurrying from one commitment to another, striving to make the most of each day's potential. However, regardless of our efforts, we all share the reality of a finite resource: time. Initially, we enter this world as time billionaires, blessed with an abundance of this precious asset at our disposal. Yet, as the years pass, time gradually slips through our fingers until we reach a point where it ceases to exist. We all face the inevitability of time's bankruptcy, encountering its depletion prior to our ultimate departure from this world.

But what if there was a way to extend our time on Earth? What if we could not only prolong our lifespan but also enhance the quality of our existence? These questions lie at the heart of the forthcoming book, "Outlive: The Science and Art of Longevity," penned by the esteemed author Peter Attia. This groundbreaking manifesto serves as both a guiding principle and an instructional manual, offering profound insights and effective strategies to help us live longer, better lives—particularly through our dietary choices.

Dr. Peter Attia, a renowned physician and expert in the field of longevity, has devoted his career to studying the science of aging and exploring methods to increase the human health span—the duration of time one can expect to live in good health. In "Outlive," Dr. Attia delves deep into the malleability of aging and lifespan, challenging conventional beliefs and sharing his own reflections while providing an in-depth examination of the science and practice of longevity.

Central to the exploration of longevity in "Outlive" is the profound impact of food and nutrition on our overall well-being and lifespan. As the saying goes, "You are what you eat," and this book offers an array of meticulously crafted recipes designed to enhance health, promote longevity, and tantalize your taste buds.

Within the pages of "Outlive Diet Recipes," you will discover a wealth of culinary delights that embody the core principles of the Outlive Diet. Our team of nutrition experts, talented chefs, and culinary enthusiasts have carefully curated a diverse range of recipes that draw inspiration from global culinary traditions. From vibrant and refreshing salads brimming with antioxidant-rich vegetables to hearty plant-based main courses that satisfy even the most discerning palates, and from comforting soups crafted from wholesome ingredients to guilt-free desserts that provide a delightful indulgence, each recipe in this collection is meticulously designed to nourish both your body and your spirit.

But this book goes far beyond a mere compilation of recipes. It serves as a comprehensive guide, offering practical tips, nutritional insights, and meal planning advice to seamlessly integrate the Outlive Diet into your daily life. Whether you are an accomplished home cook or a novice in the kitchen, "Outlive Diet Recipes" empowers you to embark on a journey of mindful eating and conscious food choices.

As you embark on this extraordinary culinary adventure, let the recipes within these pages inspire you to make sustainable changes and unlock the secrets to outliving the transient nature of diet fads. Embrace a lifelong commitment to well-being, guided by the transformative power of nourishing your body and soul.

The Outlive Diet is not a quick fix; it is a journey—a journey towards optimal health, vitality, and longevity. Through this book, we invite you to explore the potential for a vibrant and healthy future—one in which your relationship with food becomes one of nourishment, pleasure, and empowerment.

So, take a moment to inhale deeply, open your heart, and prepare yourself for an immersive experience within the realm of "Outlive Diet Recipes." Let the extraordinary flavors, vibrant colors, and tantalizing aromas transport you to a place where every bite is a step closer to well-being. May each recipe ignite your passion for cooking, nurture your body, and invigorate your spirit.

With "Outlive Diet Recipes" as your trusted companion, embark on this extraordinary journey towards a life filled with vitality, joy, and longevity. Let these recipes be the guiding light that illuminates your path to well-being and nourishes every aspect of your being.

Please note: While we strive to provide accurate nutritional information for each recipe, it is essential to acknowledge that specific calorie counts, protein, carbohydrate, and fat values may vary depending on factors such as brand, ingredient quality, and portion sizes. We encourage you to consult reliable nutrition databases or nutrition tracking apps for personalized and precise information tailored to your specific ingredients and serving sizes. By utilizing these resources, you can make well-informed choices that align with your dietary goals and preferences.

As you explore the recipes in this book, keep in mind that individual dietary needs and challenges vary. Therefore, we have incorporated personalized dietary and lifestyle recommendations throughout these pages to help you unlock your full potential and achieve optimum health. Embrace the opportunity to customize these recipes to suit your preferences and requirements, and discover a new way of living based on the latest scientific research, philosophy, and methodology.

If you are ready to take control of your well-being and strive for a longer, more fulfilling life, "Outlive Diet Recipes" is your perfect starting point. Immerse yourself in the inspiring narrative of hope, empowerment, and the transformative power of food as you navigate towards your own unique health and wellness goals.

Thank you once again for embarking on this incredible journey with us. Let the adventure begin, and may you savor the abundance of health, happiness, and longevity that awaits you on the Outlive Diet path.

PROBIOTIC-RICH FOODS

YOGURT

To obtain a generous amount of enzymes and probiotics, active culture yogurt is the optimal choice. However, it is crucial to ensure that the yogurt you purchase is pure and free from artificial sweeteners, flavors, and sugar. Before buying a carton, carefully examine the label of your chosen brand.

KEFIR

The term "kefir" originates from the Turkish word "Keyik," which conveys a sense of well-being after consumption. Kefir is a blend of goat milk, abundant in bifidobacteria and lactobacilli, and kefir grains made from yeast and bacteria. For those with lactose intolerance, coconut kefir serves as a non-dairy alternative, providing antioxidants.

KOMBUCHA TEA

This age-old brewed black or green tea has gained recognition for its weight-reducing properties and should be incorporated into your diet. Tea contains polyphenols, which contribute to a positive sense of well-being.

TEMPEH

Tempeh, a fermented soy product, serves as an excellent protein and amino acid source for vegetarians. It is also rich in Vitamin B-12.

CULTURED CONDIMENTS

You can prepare lacto-fermented condiments such as mayonnaise, mustard, salad dressing, guacamole, hot sauce, horseradish chutney, fruit chutney, and salsa. Some fermented products may lose their probiotic content during processing, but it can be reintroduced later.

PICKLED VEGETABLES

Pickling enhances the flavors of fruits and vegetables. Unpasteurized foods pickled in brine are abundant in probiotics. When selecting pickles from counters, carefully read the labels to ensure they are not cured in vinegar.

BROCCOLI

Broccoli is an exceptional Outlived food due to its high Vitamin K content, which enhances cognitive abilities, and its "choline" content, which aids in memory. Folic acid found in broccoli helps prevent depression and delays the onset of Alzheimer's disease.

Sauerkraut:
"Sauerkraut" translates to "sour cabbage" in German. This fermented cabbage nourishes healthy gut bacteria and is a valuable source of choline, which supports the healthy transmission of nervous impulses in our nervous system.

FERMENTED MEAT AND POULTRY

Make it a point to include fermented meat, fish, and eggs in your daily diet.

CHICORY ROOT AND RAW LEEKS

When consumed in their raw form, chicory root and leeks serve as an excellent source of antioxidants, effectively eliminating toxins and free radicals.

RAW GARLIC

Garlic is a true blessing for the body. Not only does it offer numerous benefits, but when eaten raw, it also provides a substantial dose of probiotics.

ACACIA GUM

Packed with probiotic fiber, Acacia gum is highly beneficial for promoting a healthy gut. Just a tablespoon of Acacia gum powder supplies the body with 6g of insoluble fiber.

DANDELION GREENS AND ASPARAGUS

Raw greens, such as dandelion greens and asparagus, are fantastic sources of probiotics. Make it a habit to include these greens in your grocery shopping each week and add them to salads or incorporate them into your meals. You can also enjoy fermented asparagus as a side dish.

ONION

Whether consumed raw or cooked, onions are impressively rich in probiotics.

RAW ARTICHOKE

Jerusalem artichokes, in addition to their probiotic content, are packed with iron and potassium. Savor them in salads.

FOOD WITHOUT GLUTEN

HEALTHY FAT

Include the following in your diet to incorporate healthy fats: coconut oil, almond milk, extra virgin olive oil, sesame oil, coconuts, nuts, flax seeds, chia seeds, pumpkin seeds, cheese, sesame seeds, sunflower seeds, ghee, nut butter, and avocados.

PROTEIN

For a good source of protein, consider including the following in your meals: eggs, poultry, shellfish, wild fish such as mahi-mahi, trout, herring, salmon, grouper, black cod, sardines, liver, chicken, turkey, veal, duck, lamb, bison, beef, ostrich, lobsters, crabs, and mollusks.

LEAFY VEGETABLES

Boost your nutrient intake with leafy vegetables like lettuce, kale, cabbage, horseradish, collard greens, spinach, onions, cauliflower, chard, mushrooms, turnips, watercress, asparagus, celery, shallots, jicama, Brussels sprouts, ginger, leek, beans, radishes, and parsley.

FRUITS

Incorporate low-sugar fruits into your daily diet. Some examples include lime, cucumber, pumpkin, lemon, squash, bell peppers, avocado, and eggplants.

CONDIMENTS AND SEASONINGS

You can enjoy a variety of seasonings and condiments that are free from soy, gluten, sugar, and wheat. Mustard and salsa are good options to enhance flavor.

GLUTTON FREE PRODUCTS

In addition to the above, you can consume the following food products in moderation: yogurt, kefir, blueberries, carrots, parsnips, beans, lentils, buckwheat, oats, quinoa, rice, and one glass of red wine a day, which is rich in polyphenols and beneficial for gut health.

CONDIMENTS AND SEASONINGS

You can enjoy a variety of seasonings and condiments that are free from soy, gluten, sugar, and wheat. Mustard and salsa are good options to enhance flavor.

GLUTTON FREE PRODUCTS

In addition to the above, you can consume the following food products in moderation: yogurt, kefir, blueberries, carrots, parsnips, beans, lentils, buckwheat, oats, quinoa, rice, and one glass of red wine a day, which is rich in polyphenols and beneficial for gut health.

STAY HYDRATED

Keeping yourself well hydrated is crucial for gut health. Avoid tap water that contains chlorine, as it can be harmful to the microbial environment in your gut. Opt for mineral or filtered water to support the flourishing of your gut microbiome.

REDUCE
ANTIBIOTIC USAGE

In our pursuit of quick remedies, even for minor ailments like the common cold and fever, we often rush to local clinics where we are prescribed broad-spectrum antibiotics. However, it's important to be mindful that these broad-spectrum antibiotics not only target harmful bacteria but also eliminate beneficial gut bacteria.

The gut microbes play a vital role in safeguarding the gut lining and reducing its permeability. By doing so, they help lower the risk of inflammation throughout our bodies. Unfortunately, the excessive use of antibiotics and exposure to environmental toxins can disrupt the balance of these microbes and harm the integrity of the gut lining. Inflammation, which underlies serious conditions such as Alzheimer's, dementia, diabetes, and cancer, can be attributed to these disruptions.

Recognizing the significance of protecting our gut bacteria and understanding its pivotal role in maintaining our overall health can significantly contribute to the treatment and prevention of debilitating neurological diseases.

THE MEDITERRANEAN DIET

The Mediterranean diet emphasizes the consumption of seafood, fruits, vegetables, nuts, whole grains, and olive oil. These nourishing foods are known to ward off diseases such as diabetes, coronary conditions, cancer, and cognitive decline. A strong commitment to this anti-inflammatory diet has been linked to improved cognitive function, reduced risk of Alzheimer's disease, and slower deterioration of brain function. Although transitioning from indulgent and addictive junk food to a healthier alternative may require some effort, it can make a significant difference in our overall well-being.

The emerging understanding of the gut-brain connection has paved the way for intriguing experiments. A growing body of evidence supports the notion that a Mediterranean diet, abundant in antioxidants found in berries and fruits, can enhance brain function. These antioxidants help combat the damaging effects of free radicals and contribute to the prevention of neurodegeneration. Furthermore, reducing the intake of sugars, fried foods, red meat, and carbohydrates plays a vital role in maintaining brain health.

Incorporating olive oil and nuts into our diet is also beneficial for brain health. These foods contain polyphenols, which act as safeguards against oxidation and inflammation—both of which are harmful to the blood vessels in the brain. Since the brain relies heavily on oxygen, clogged blood vessels can lead to the destruction of brain cells. Polyphenols can also be found in plant-based products like berries, tea, and spices such as turmeric (curcuma).

MEDITERRANEAN DIET FOR BEGINNERS

Tips for Starting a Mediterranean Diet:

1. **Prioritize Vegetables:** Stock up on a variety of vegetables for your meals. Whether it's a simple salad of cherry tomatoes with olive oil and feta cheese, a vegetable-loaded pizza replacing pepperoni and sausage, vegetable soups, or side dishes at restaurants, make sure to incorporate ample veggies.

2. **Reduce Meat Consumption:** If you're a meat lover, consider reevaluating your dietary choices. Try reducing portion sizes and opt for leaner cuts. One way to include meat in a healthy dish is by adding chunks of chicken or fish to a leafy salad for extra flavor.

3. **Don't Skip Breakfast:** Avoid the mistake of skipping breakfast, especially when short on time. Choose fruits, breakfast cereals, whole grain wheat, or fiber-rich foods to kick-start your day in a healthy way. A nutritious breakfast will keep you fuller for longer and help curb calorie cravings.

4. **Increase Seafood Intake:** Aim to consume seafood rich in omega-3 fatty acids at least twice a week. Fish such as shellfish, tuna, herring, salmon, sardines, and oysters are excellent choices. Grilling fish with olive oil and serving it alongside green beans makes for a delicious and hearty meal.

5. **Choose Healthy Fats:** Incorporate good fats into your diet, such as olive oil, nuts, olives, sunflower seeds, flax seeds, and avocados. These fats contribute to maintaining gut health. Sunflower, soybean, and corn oil are also sources of polyunsaturated fats.

6. **Include Dairy:** Integrate yogurt, Greek yogurt, cheese, and milk into your daily diet. Opt for low-fat dairy products from the counter.

7. **Opt for Fruits over Desserts:** Instead of high-carb desserts, satisfy your occasional sweet tooth with fresh fruits. You can also cut up fruits and mix them with low-fat yogurt to create your own flavored yogurt at home.

GUT HEALTH AND THE MEDITERRANEAN DIET

Our diet plays a significant role in shaping our gut microbiota. A Mediterranean dietary style exhibits several characteristics that positively influence gut health, including a beneficial fatty acid profile, high antioxidant intake, focus on polyunsaturated and monounsaturated fatty acids, and the presence of high-fiber, low-glycemic index foods.

Carbohydrates and Digestion: The challenging nature of carbohydrates is a leading cause of obesity worldwide. Our bodies are not well adapted to digesting excessive amounts of polysaccharide molecules. By reducing the consumption of carbohydrate-rich foods, we are more likely to maintain a healthy weight and promote gut microbiota health.

Increased Fiber Consumption: Fiber has numerous health benefits, such as decreasing the absorption of sugar and cholesterol in the gut, promoting the production of phytochemicals and other bioactive compounds, and possessing anti-inflammatory properties. Fermentation of fiber by the gut microbial community releases phenolic compounds that exhibit antioxidant and anti-inflammatory effects.

Abundant Antioxidants: The Mediterranean diet includes an abundance of fresh fruits, which are rich in antioxidants. Research has shown that consuming fresh fruits significantly increases the presence of beneficial bacteria such as Lactobacilli and bifidobacteria, which are associated with maintaining gut health.

Restriction of Fat: Apart from aiding in weight management, a diet low in fat creates a favorable environment for the growth of Lactobacilli and bifidobacteria. Conversely, a high-fat diet is linked to an increased risk of obesity-related gut wall permeability and subsequent inflammation.

Our diet plays a significant role in shaping our gut microbiota. A Mediterranean dietary style exhibits several characteristics that positively influence gut health, including a beneficial fatty acid profile, high antioxidant intake, focus on polyunsaturated and monounsaturated fatty acids, and the presence of high-fiber, low-glycemic index foods.

Carbohydrates and Digestion: The challenging nature of carbohydrates is a leading cause of obesity worldwide. Our bodies are not well adapted to digesting excessive amounts of polysaccharide molecules. By reducing the consumption of carbohydrate-rich foods, we are more likely to maintain a healthy weight and promote gut microbiota health.

Increased Fiber Consumption: Fiber has numerous health benefits, such as decreasing the absorption of sugar and cholesterol in the gut, promoting the production of phytochemicals and other bioactive compounds, and possessing anti-inflammatory properties. Fermentation of fiber by the gut microbial community releases phenolic compounds that exhibit antioxidant and anti-inflammatory effects.

Abundant Antioxidants: The Mediterranean diet includes an abundance of fresh fruits, which are rich in antioxidants. Research has shown that consuming fresh fruits significantly increases the presence of beneficial bacteria such as Lactobacilli and bifidobacteria, which are associated with maintaining gut health.

Restriction of Fat: Apart from aiding in weight management, a diet low in fat creates a favorable environment for the growth of Lactobacilli and bifidobacteria. Conversely, a high-fat diet is linked to an increased risk of obesity-related gut wall permeability and subsequent inflammation.

WHO CAN BENEFIT FROM THESE RECIPES?

These recipes cater to a wide range of individuals seeking to enhance brain health, improve gut ecology, lose weight, and lead a healthy lifestyle. Specifically, these recipes are ideal for those looking for:

- Brain Healthy Recipes

- Mediterranean Recipes

- Anti-Inflammatory Recipes

- Immune system Boosting Recipes

- Diabetic-Friendly Recipes

- Low-Sugar Recipes

- Gluten-Free Recipes

- Low-Carb Recipes

- Anti-Inflammatory Recipes

- Protein-rich Recipes

- Soy-Free Recipes

LET'S BEGIN

Welcome to the captivating realm of Outlive Diet Recipes! Here, you'll discover a collection of healthy and delightful recipes that promote longevity, improve gut ecology, and enhance overall health. These culinary wonders will leave you looking and feeling younger, empowering you to embrace a long and healthy life.

Each recipe offers a simple method of preparation, and you can easily make substitutions or personalize them to suit your preferences and circumstances.

While I've put considerable effort into perfecting these recipes, I welcome your feedback if you spot any errors. Please reach out to me at giovandylan@gmail.com.

The moment has arrived to embark upon a magnificent expedition of crafting nourishing, straightforward, and scrumptious recipes. May fortune smile upon your culinary endeavors, and may you revel in the utmost success and delight!

Without further ado, let us dive deep into the enchanting world of these extraordinary recipes!

PART I: BREAKFAST

VANILLA CHERRY QUINOA

Calorie Content per Serving: Approximately 350–400 calories

Preparation Time: 20 Minutes
Serves: 2

Ingredients:

- 1.5 cups water

- 3/4 cup dry Quinoa

- 3/4 cup unsweetened, dried cherries

- 2 tsp Vanilla Extract

- 1 – 2 pinch ground Cinnamon

Optional – Raw Honey, to taste

How you make it:

1. In a medium-sized saucepan, combine the water, dry quinoa, unsweetened dried cherries, vanilla extract, and ground cinnamon (exclude the raw honey).

2. Place the saucepan over a medium-high flame and bring the mixture to a boil.

3. Once the mixture reaches a boil, reduce the heat to low, cover the pan, and allow the

contents to simmer for approximately 15 minutes or until the water has been completely absorbed and the quinoa is soft. Stir occasionally.

4. Remove the saucepan from the heat and transfer the cooked quinoa mixture into bowls.

5. If desired, drizzle the quinoa with raw honey for added sweetness.

6. Serve and enjoy!

Note: The optional honey can be added according to personal preference for additional sweetness.

Please note: that the calorie content provided is an estimate and may vary depending on the specific brands and quantities of ingredients used. Adjustments or additions to the recipe, such as the optional honey, will affect the overall calorie count.

CHICK PEAS AND POTATO HASH

Calorie Content per Serving: Approximately 350–400 calories

This hash recipe from Eating Well is a great choice for any time of the day, but it offers specific benefits when enjoyed for breakfast. One of its notable advantages is its ability to provide a satisfying feeling of fullness and energize you for the day ahead. Each serving contains approximately 14 grams of protein and 6 grams of fiber. This quantity is ample to serve a group of 4 individuals.

Ingredients:

- 4 cups frozen shredded hash brown potatoes

- 2 cups finely chopped baby spinach

- ½ cup finely chopped onion

- 1 tablespoon minced fresh ginger

- 1 tablespoon curry powder

- 1/2 teaspoon salt

- 1/4 cup extra-virgin olive oil

- 1 (15-ounce) can chickpeas, rinsed

- 1 cup chopped zucchini

- 4 large eggs

How you make it:

The directions for this recipe are very simple. All you have to do is:

1. Combine potatoes, spinach, onion, ginger, curry powder, and salt in a large bowl.

2. Now take a large non-stick pan and heat some oil in it over medium-high heat.

3. Now add the potato mixture and press into a layer. Make sure you cook without stirring for an approximate time of 3 to 5 minutes.

4. Keep on cooking until the potatoes become crispy and golden brown on the bottom.

5. Now reduce the heat to a medium-low level. Fold in chickpeas and zucchini, and break the large chunks of potatoes until they are thoroughly combined.

6. Now, press them back properly into another layer. Carve out 4 holes in the mixture.

7. Now break the eggs in such a way that one egg is broken at a time. Put them all in a cup and after mixing them, just pour them into each of the indentations.

8. Also, again cover the pan and keep on cooking until the eggs are set. In case you are interested in soft- set yolks, you should cook them for a maximum period of 4 to 5 minutes.

AVOCADO TOAST

For a delicious and healthy breakfast, try this amazing recipe that will help you maintain a wholesome lifestyle. To make the most of this dish, it's important to choose whole grain bread, which aligns with a Mediterranean diet. This diet emphasizes fresh flavors and often incorporates generous amounts of herbs for a refreshing taste and aroma. If you prefer an alternative to bread, rye can be used as a suitable substitute. Check out the list of ingredients below to prepare the avocado toast:

Ingredients:

- 2 small firm-ripe avocados, that are peeled, and the seed is removed

- 80 grams of soft feta which is crumbled

- 2 tablespoons chopped fresh mint, plus extra to garnish

- squeeze fresh lemon juice, to taste

- 4 large slices of rye bread

How you make it:

1. Place the avocado in a medium sized bowl and mash it roughly with a fork.

2. Now add some mint to the mixture along with a squeeze of the lemon juice.

3. Mix them properly until a homogeneous mixture is formed. Now that a thorough mixture has been prepared, season it with sea salt and freshly ground black pepper which is going to add to the taste and the flavor of the dish.

4. Now coming towards the rye bread, toast it or grill it until it becomes golden in color.

5. In order to serve, put 1/4th of the avocado mixture on each slice of the bread. In order to enhance the flavoring, top it with feta.

RASPBERRY GREEN TEA POWER SMOOTHIE

Preparation Time: 10 Minutes

Serves: 2

Ingredients:

- 2 cups Green Tea – chilled

- 1 large cup of Raspberries, frozen

- 1 small Banana

- 2 scoops Protein powder

- 2 tsp raw Honey

How you make it:

1. In a blender, combine all the ingredients: chilled green tea, frozen raspberries, banana, protein powder, and raw honey.

2. Blend the ingredients until you achieve a smooth and creamy puree.

3. Pour the smoothie into tall glasses.

4. Enjoy the refreshing and nourishing Raspberry Green Tea Power Smoothie!

SWEET SPICED OATS

Calorie Content per Serving: Approximately 200–250 calories

Preparation Time: 10 Minutes

Serves: 2

Ingredients:

- 2 cups Water

- 1 cup Oats

- 1/2 cup dried Cranberries / Cherries

- 1 tsp Cinnamon powder

- 1 tsp Nutmeg powder

- 2 tbsp. Molasses

- 2 tbsp. Flaxseeds

How you make it:

1. In a small saucepan, combine the water, oats, dried cranberries or cherries, cinnamon powder, and nutmeg powder.

2. Bring the mixture to a boil over medium-high heat.

3. Once the mixture boils, reduce the heat, cover the saucepan, and allow it to simmer for about 5 minutes or until all the water is absorbed and the oats are cooked to your desired consistency.

4. Stir in the flaxseeds and cover the saucepan for an additional 5 minutes off the heat.

5. Drizzle the sweet spiced oats with molasses.

6. Serve and enjoy the warm and comforting Sweet Spiced Oats.

SWEET AND SAVOURY BREAKFAST MUFFINS

Calorie Content per Serving: Approximately 150–200 calories

Preparation Time: 30 minutes

Serves: 4 – 6

Ingredients:

3 cups All-Purpose Flour

1 cup stevia or brown sugar

2 tsp Baking Powder

1 pinch of Salt

1.5 tsp Cinnamon powder

1.5 tsp Ginger – ground.

1 cup Almond milk (unsweetened)

2 Apples – shredded

1/3 cup mashed, ripe Banana

1.5 tbsp. Apple Cider vinegar

1/3 cup Crystallised ginger – finely chopped

How you make it:

1. Preheat the oven to 400°F (200°C). Lightly grease a muffin pan or line it with muffin liners (a 12-cup pan should suffice).

2. In a medium bowl, whisk together the flour, stevia or brown sugar, baking powder, salt, and spices to create the flour mixture.

3. In another bowl, mix the almond milk, mashed banana, shredded apples, apple cider vinegar, and crystallized ginger.

4. Add the flour mixture to the wet ingredients and stir until you have a consistent batter.

5. Pour the batter into the muffin pan or liners, filling each cup about 2/3 full.

6. Bake the muffins in the preheated oven at 400°F (200°C) for about 15-20 minutes or until a toothpick inserted into the center comes out clean.

7. Remove the muffins from the oven and allow them to cool slightly before serving.

MEDITERRANEAN FRITTATA

Calorie Content per Serving: Approximately 250–300 calories

While consuming vegetables for breakfast may not initially appear enticing, incorporating them into a frittata can transform it into a delectable morning recipe. Enhance the flavor and taste of your baked egg breakfast by including a few additional ingredients. For instance, onions, red peppers, and olives are viable options. Additionally, you can experiment with various types of peppers. This recipe yields six servings, making it ideal for a group of people.

Ingredients:

- 1 cup chopped onion

- 2 cloves minced garlic

- 3 tablespoons olive oil

- 8 eggs- beaten

- 1/4 cup light cream or milk

- 1/2 cup crumbled feta cheese (2 ounces)

- 1/2 cup chopped bottled roasted red sweet peppers

- 1/2 cup sliced pitted ripe olives (optional)

- 1/4 cup slivered fresh basil

- 1/8 teaspoon ground black pepper

- 1/2 cup onion and coarsely crushed garlic croutons

- 2 tablespoons finely shredded Parmesan cheese

- Fresh basil leaves (optional)

How you make it:

1. The first step is to preheat the broiler. In a large skillet cook onion and garlic in approximately 2 tablespoons of hot oil.

2. Make sure you keep on heating it until the onions become tender. While this part of cooking is in the process, you should simultaneously beat the eggs together in a bowl.

3. Now that you have beaten the eggs properly, stir in some feta cheese and roasted sweet pepper.

4. You can add olives also but that is optional. You can add them if desired. After this, add some basil and black pepper.

5. Now that a complete mixture is being prepared, pour it over the onion mixture that is being cooked in the skillet.

6. After pouring it, cook it over a medium-heat flame. After heating for a little while the mixture will set.

7. When this happens, run a spatula around the edge of the skillet so that the egg mixture is lifted and the uncooked portion flows underneath.

8. Continue doing this until the egg mixture is completely set.

9. You will realize that it is completely cooked when the surface gets a little moist.

10. Once this point is reached, just reduce the intensity of the flame in order to prevent overcooking.

11. Now take another bowl and add crushed croutons, parmesan cheese, and the remaining tablespoons of oil. Sprinkle this mixture over the frittata.

12. Make sure the top is set and the crumbs are golden. Cut this frittata in wedges and serve them right away.

13. If you wish to garnish it then you can even do that with fresh basil leaves.

QUINOA BUCKWHEAT FLAPJACKS

Calorie Content per Serving: Approximately 250–300 calories

Preparation Time: 1 Hour

Serves: 3 – 4

Ingredients:

4 Tbsp. raw Honey

4 Tbsp. cold pressed Coconut Oil

2 tsp Vanilla Extract

1/4 tsp Cinnamon powder

1/4 tsp Ginger – ground

1 cup Quinoa – cooked

1 cup Buckwheat grout

1 cup Oats

1 cup dried Cranberries

How you make it:

1. Preheat the oven to 325oF.

2. Grease a baking pan, line it with a parchment sheet, and put it aside.

3. Mix the coconut oil, honey, vanilla, cinnamon, and ginger in a small bowl.

4. In a large bowl, combine together the Buckwheat, Cranberries, Quinoa and Oats.

5. Add the mixture from the small bowl and stir vigorously to combine.

6. Spread this mixture onto the baking pan in an even, uniform layer.

7. Place the baking tray in the oven and bake at 325oF for about 45.

8. minutes until the grains start to brown. Remove the baking tray from the oven and place on a wire rack to cool.

9. Cut into bite-sized pieces and store in an airtight container.

ORIENTAL BAKED OMELETS

Preparation Time: 1 hour

SERVES: 6

Ingredients:

- 500 gm sliced Button Mushrooms

- 2 medium Onions, chopped

- 2 tbsp. Garlic, finely chopped

- 500 gm Fresh Spinach leaves, roughly chopped.

- ½ cup Water

- 6 Egg Whites

- 4 large Eggs

- 5 oz. Tofu

- 1 – 2 pinch Turmeric powder Salt and Pepper to taste.

How you make it:

1. Preheat the oven to 350oF. Sauté the mushrooms in a lightly greased oven-proof skillet or pan until the mushrooms are golden brown.

2. To this, add the onions and cook till they are soft. Add the chopped garlic to this and cook for another 20 seconds.

3. Add the spinach and water, and cook with the lid on for about 2 minutes until the spinach wilts. Remove the lid and cook further until the water has evaporated.

4. In a blender, add the tofu, egg whites and egg with the turmeric powder, salt and pepper and blend till smooth. Pour this egg mixture gently over the spinach and mushrooms.

5. Transfer the pan to the oven and bake for about 20 minutes at 350oF so that the eggs are set in the center.

6. Remove the pan from the oven and invert over a plate and allow to cool. Cut the omelet into wedges and serve!

NUTTY PROTEIN OATS

Calorie Content per Serving: Approximately 300—400 calories

Preparation Time: 1 hour

Serves: 3 – 4

Ingredients:

- 4 cups Water

- 1 cup Steel Cut Oats

- 3 tsp Pumpkin Pie Spice

- 10 scoops Protein powder

- 1.5 cup Apple Sauce

- 1 tsp raw Honey/Agave/Stevia extract

- 15 – 20 Pecans or Walnuts

How you make it:

1. In a saucepan, bring the water to a boil and stir in the steel-cut oats with the pumpkin pie spice and allow this to cook for 5 minutes.

2. Lower the heat and allow this to simmer for another 30 minutes and take off the flame.

3. Let the mixture cool and then stir in the protein powder.

4. This recipe can be prepared the night before, stored in the fridge and warmed up in the microwave in the morning.

5. Add the rest of the ingredients when you are ready to eat!

6. If this is prepared the night before, then remove the oats from the fridge and serve in individual bowls.

7. Divide the remaining ingredients between the bowls and stir well. Microwave for about 2 minutes on high, stirring every 30 seconds and serve hot!

BAKED CHEESY EGGS

Preparation Time: 1 hour

Serves: 2

Ingredients:

8 Roma Tomatoes, peeled and chopped into small pieces

2 tbsp. Olive Oil

2 tbsp. Vegetable stock

1 medium Onion – finely chopped

100 gm Beef – roughly chopped

150gm Spinach – chopped

5 large Egg Whites

1/4 cup Cream Cheese (can substitute with dairy free cheese too)

1/4 small cup of fresh Chives – chopped

4 tbsp. Almond milk – unsweetened

How you make it:

1. Preheat the oven to 350oF. Coat the inner surface of two oven-safe bowls with olive oil or any other organic virgin oil.

2. In a separate bowl, toss together the tomatoes and salt. Spoon this content between the two greased bowls, and set them aside.

3. In another large skillet, add oil and then onions. Once the onions are translucent, add vegetable stock and cook over a medium heat, stirring occasionally for 4 minutes.

4. Add the chopped beef and cook for another minute more, and remove the pan from the heat.

5. Add the spinach and toss lightly in the ham and onion mixture to wilt the leaves lightly and then add this to the two bowls with the tomatoes.

6. In another bowl, whisk the egg whites, cream cheese, chopped chives and almond milk. Add this to the bowls having the tomato mixture.

7. Place the bowls on a baking tray or pan that is large enough to hold both of them and place the tray on the middle rack in the oven.

8. Pour boiling water carefully onto the pan so that the bowls are submerged about half way. Bake them for about 30 minutes.

9. Once done, remove the bowls carefully from the tray and season with salt and pepper, serve hot.

10. You can optionally garnish the dish with orange slices for an extra burst of flavor.

BERRY NUT BURST

Calorie Content per Serving: Approximately 150—200 calories

Preparation Time: 5 Minutes

Serves: 2

Ingredients:

- 2 cups Strawberries

- 1.5 cup Blueberries

- 1.4 cup Walnuts and Pecans (roughly chopped)

- 2 cups fat-free Greek Yogurt

How you make it:

1. Mix the berries and nuts into the yogurt, scoop into bowls.

2. Garnish with a mint leaf and serve!

PROVOLONE EGG WHITE OMELETS

Preparation Time: 15 Minutes

Serves: 2

Ingredients:

- 2 tbsp. Olive oil

- 1/2 cup Onions – diced

- 1/2 cup Green Peppers – diced

- 1/2 cup Garbanzo Beans – canned

- 1 cup Egg whites

- 1 cup Salsa

- 2 slices low fat Provolone Cheese

- 1/2 cup Mandarin – sliced, in water Seasoning -

- Basil

- Oregano

- Salt & Pepper

How you make it:

1. In a pan, add 2 tbsp. of olive oil and heat. To this, add the peppers and onions until they have softened.

2. Drain the Garbanzo beans, rinse thoroughly and slightly mash them.

3. Add the beans to the pan and sauté gently.

4. In a bowl, beat the egg whites till they are lightly foamy. Add the spices to this, and whisk lightly once again.

5. Gently pour the egg whites over the cooking beans, onions and peppers making sure you cover the whole pan.

6. Add the cheese, cover and let the eggs cook on a low medium heat until the cheese is melted and the eggs are cooked.

7. Serve onto a plate, fold in half and top with the salsa. You can add the mandarin slices as a garnish, or serve it as an accompaniment for a wonderful breakfast.

CURRIED APPLE CHUTNEY

Makes about 6 cups

This is a tasty side dish that you can enjoy with just about any main course. Choose a firm variety of apples, such as Granny Smith, Rome Beauty, Honeycrisp, Golden Delicious, Empire, Northern Spy, or Pink Lady. If you prefer, you can substitute firm peaches or pears instead of apples.

Ingredients:

- 6 cups sliced apples (apple pie size)

- 1/2 cup whey or water kefir

- 1/2 cup lemon juice

- 1/4 cup stevia (or more, to taste)

- 1 teaspoon sea salt

- 4 teaspoons mild curry powder

Optional: 1 cup raisins, 1 cup chopped celery, or 1 cup sliced green bell pepper (each provides an additional sweet or savory taste)

How you make it:

1. Mix all ingredients in a bowl and taste to ensure the proportions are about right for you (add more of anything as needed).

2. Transfer to a jar, crock, or other container, and cover loosely.

3. You may like this a little sweet or with a stronger sour taste; start tasting it after one day and be prepared to give it 2–4 days to ferment.

4. Once it is ready, cover the container tightly and store it in the refrigerator for up to two weeks.

PART II: LUNCH

PASTA ORZO AND TOMATOES

Calorie Content per Serving: Approximately 350–400 calories

Preparation Time: 20 minutes

SERVES: 1 – 2

Ingredients:

- 1 cup Orzo pasta

- 2 tsp Onion Flakes - dehydrated

- 1/2 tsp Chili Powder

-
- 1/2 tsp Oregano – roughly ground

- 1/2 tsp Cumin

- 1/2 tsp Garlic - Powdered

- 1/2 tsp Cayenne Pepper - (optional)

- 1/2 cup Tomatoes – canned or fresh, with tomato sauce

- 1 tsp Lime Juice – fresh

- 3 tsp. Extra Virgin olive oil Salt - to taste

How you make it:

1. Prepare the pasta as per instructions, drain and keep aside.

2. In a medium saucepan, add the olive oil and sauté the onions till soft.

3. To this add the spices and allow the mixture to cook on medium heat till the oil leaves the mixture.

4. Add the lime juice and allow to cook for a further 30 seconds.

5. Add the pasta to the mixture, tossing gently to ensure that the pasta is evenly coated.

6. Serve on plates and garnish with the dehydrated onion flakes. Enjoy!

7. You can also replace the Orzo with any other small-sized pasta of your choice!

DELICIOUS CHICKEN AND CUCUMBER SALAD

Calorie Content per Serving: Approximately 350–400 calories

To serve this salad, it is recommended to accompany it with pita wedges or pita chips. You have the option of either purchasing ready-made pita chips or making your own. To make your own, lightly spray the pita wedges with cooking spray and sprinkle a small amount of shredded parmesan cheese on top. Bake them at 400 degrees Fahrenheit for approximately 10 minutes.

Ingredients:

- 2 cups chopped cooked chicken breast

- 1¬ 1/4 cups chopped seeded cucumber

- 1/2 cup matchstick-cut carrots

- 1/2 cup sliced radishes

- 1/3 cup chopped green onions

- 1/4 cup light mayonnaise

- 2 tablespoons chopped fresh cilantro

- 1 teaspoon bottled minced garlic

- 1/4 teaspoon salt

- 1/4 teaspoon ground cumin

- 1/8 teaspoon black pepper

- 4 green leaf lettuce leaves

- 4 (6-inch) whole wheat pitas, each cut into 8 wedges

How you make it:

1. Combine the chopped and cooked chicken breast along with chopped seeded cucumber, carrots, radishes, and green onions in a large bowl.

2. Combine mayonnaise and fresh cilantro, minced garlic, salt, ground cumin and black pepper in another comparatively small bowl. Keep on stirring with a whisk.

3. The next step is to add the mayonnaise mixture to the chicken mixture and keep on stirring until they are properly mixed.

4. Place 1 lettuce leaf on each of 4 plates; top each leaf with about 1 cup of chicken mixture. Also, place 8 pita wedges with each serving plate. This recipe contains 382 calories.

AVOCADO, TURKEY, BLACK BEAN AND CHEESE SALAD

Preparation Time: 20 minutes

Serves: 2

Ingredients:

- 2/3 cup canned Black Beans - rinsed/drained

- 1 Yellow Bell Pepper - diced

- 2 cups Cucumber - chopped

- 1.5 cups Red Onions - diced

- 1 Avocado - diced

- 1/2 tsp Ground Cumin

- 1-2 tbsp. Balsamic Vinegar

- 1-2 tbsp. Lime juice – freshly squeezed

- ¼ cup Parsley - chopped Oregano - fresh chopped or 1tsp dried – to season

- Salt and pepper - to taste

- Tabasco Sauce - to taste

- 1 cup Turkey breast – diced and shredded

- 1/2 cup Monterey Jack cheese – Low Fat, Shredded

How you make it:

1. Add all the ingredients except the cheese in a bowl and mix well. Season with Tabasco sauce, salt and pepper and toss well.

2. Sprinkle the Monterey Jack cheese on top, and serve at room temperature or chilled.

Instructions:

1. Combine all ingredients except the shredded cheese in a bowl, adding Tabasco sauce and salt and pepper to taste.

2. Toss well. Sprinkle the shredded Colby Jack on top. Serve at room temperature or chilled.

NOURISHING KIMCHI NOODLES

Calorie Content per Serving: Approximately 150–250 calories

Makes 1–2 servings

This recipe begins with your favorite noodles. Wheat noodles, either Asian or Western types, work best. Spaghetti, fettuccini, macaroni, or any raw food substitute should be fine.

Ingredients:

- 2 cups cooked noodles

- 1/2–1 cup kimchi, chopped

- 1 teaspoon toasted sesame oil

- 1 teaspoon sesame seeds

- 1/2 cucumber, sliced lengthwise into thin ribbons that resemble noodles Soy sauce or salt to taste

Optional: 1 sheet of sushi seaweed

How you make it:

1. Put freshly cooked noodles in a bowl, add other ingredients, and stir.

2. This actually is a great cold dish, but if you need to warm them up, then stir-fry the noodles first in a little cooking oil on a skillet.

3. While they are still warm, but no longer scalding hot, transfer to a bowl, then add other ingredients and stir.

4. If you use the optional sheet of sushi seaweed, then crumble this over the top of your dish at the last minute just before eating.

BBQ CHICKEN SALAD

Preparation Time: 20 Minutes

SERVES: 1 - 2

Ingredients:

- 3 tbsp. cold pressed Olive Oil

- 1 large Chicken breast – boneless and diced

- 1 large Bell pepper – cut into strips

- 1 medium Onion – diced

- ½ tsp Cider Vinegar

- 1.2 tsp Worcestershire Sauce

- 6 cloves Garlic – finely minced

-
- 4 tbsp. Barbeque sauce

- 1 Bag Lettuce/Salad greens

- ½ bag Coleslaw Mix / Shredded Cabbage

- Salt and pepper – for seasoning

How you make it:

1. In a medium saucepan, add the olive oil and sauté the bell peppers, onion, and garlic till soft. Add the vinegar and Worcestershire sauce and sauté for a further 30 seconds.

2. Add the chicken breast and the barbeque sauce and mix gently.

3. Cover and allow this to simmer on low heat for 5 minutes. Stir occasionally to ensure that the flavors mix well.

4. In a large bowl, toss the salad mix/lettuce with the cabbage and with plate this onto a large serving dish.

5. Add the chicken mixture to the top of the salad and season with salt and pepper.

TASTY RADISH KIMCHI

While cabbage kimchi is the most well-known, there are other types also. One particular favorite is Radish kimchi. This recipe utilizes fermented shrimp paste as a source of Lacto-bacteria, though you can substitute less authentic sources such as yogurt whey, sauerkraut juice, or vegetable culture.

Both the shrimp paste and fish stock are available at Asian grocery stores. The sea salt in this recipe is used to coat and leech fluid from the radish cubes, but it is then rinsed off, so there is no added salt in the end product. If you decide to make this side dish without fermented shrimp paste, which is salty, then you may need to add additional sea salt near the end (to suit your taste).

Ingredients:

- 2 large Korean Daikon radishes (larger than most other types), cut into 1-inch cubes

- 1 large onion, sliced or roughly chopped

- 5–7 scallions (green onions), finely chopped

- 5–7 cloves garlic

- 2 inches ginger, peeled and finely chopped

- 1/3 Cup dried red chili pepper powder

- 1/3 Cup fermented shrimp paste

- 1/3 Cup fish stock or fish sauce (such as anchovy)

- 4–5 tablespoons sea salt

- 1½ tablespoons stevia

- More salt, to taste

- Sesame seeds, to sprinkle on top

How you make it:

1. Trim Daikon radishes and cut them into cubes.

2. Place radish cubes in a bowl, add salt, and mix well.

3. Let them sit for 1 hour, during which time the salt will leech out some of the fluid.

4. After 1 hour, rinse the radishes and drain them in a colander or strainer.

5. Use a blender to combine and purée the onion, garlic, ginger, and shrimp paste with the fish stock to make a thin paste.

6. In a bowl, mix onion-garlic-ginger purée with fermented shrimp paste, fish stock, stevia, and chili pepper powder.

7. Toss this sauce mixture with the radish cubes, coating them evenly. Then stir in scallions.

8. Move radish kimchi to a large crock or jar, pouring and scraping over it any additional sauce that remains in the bowl.

9. Cover and let kimchi ferment at room temperature. It should take 2–4 days, depending on temperature, but check it every day or so and feel free to taste.

10. Once it has fermented, cover it tightly and move it to the refrigerator for storage.

11. You can keep eating it and the kimchi will last for several weeks in the fridge

BROCCOLI AND CHICKEN CASSEROLE

Preparation Time: 45 minutes

Serves: 6

Ingredients:

- 1 large bag of Salad leaves (with dressing)

- 1 large head of Broccoli (cut into 1" pieces)

- 1 large Chicken Breast (diced into 1" cubes)

- 2 tbsp. Olive oil

- 3 tbsps. Corn starch

- 2.5 cups 1% Milk

- 2-3 tbsp. Dijon mustard

- 1/2 cup Light Mayonnaise

- 1/2 cup fat-free Greek Yogurt

- 1 medium Lime – squeeze the juice

- 1 tbsp. Lemon Zest

- 3 large Tablespoons Parmesan cheese (grated)

How you make it:

1. Prepare the salad and keep it in the refrigerator to chill.

2. Preheat the oven to about 350oF.

3. In a steamer, add the broccoli and steam for 4 minutes. Collect the broccoli in a colander to drain and add this to a medium-sized baking dish.

4. Add the olive oil to a medium skillet, and add the chicken pieces to cook until each cube is a light brown color. Add in the corn starch and stir.

5. To this, slowly pour in the milk and stir till the mixture beings to boil and thicken.

6. Add the yogurt, mayonnaise, mustard, lime juice and lemon zest and stir till the chicken is coated in a uniform manner.

7. Spoon the chicken mixture over the broccoli. Sprinkle the grated cheese over the top and bake for about 15 minutes until the top browns and the mixture bubbles around the edges.

8. Serve the casserole with the salad on the side

BROCCOLI SALAD WITH BAKED CHICKEN

Preparation time: 30 Minutes

SERVES: 2

Ingredients:

- 3 tbsp. Light Mayonnaise

- 2 tbsp. low-fat plain Yogurt A pinch of Celery seed

- 1 medium Red Onion- chopped

- 1 small head of Broccoli – chopped

- 3 tbsp. dried Cranberries

- 1 cup Seedless grapes (red preferred)

- 1 tbsp. Almonds – finely sliced

- 1 large Chicken breast

- 2 tbsp. Barbeque sauce

- Pepper and Salt – to taste

How you make it:

1. Gently whisk the lemon juice, celery seed and pepper in a small bowl with the mayonnaise to make the dressing.

2. Set the dressing to chill in the refrigerator. Add the chopped broccoli to a steamer or drop into boiling water and cook till tender, but al dente. Drain the broccoli and allow cooling.

3. Add the chopped red onions, dried cranberries, almonds, and dressing to the cooked broccoli and toss well.

4. Bake or broil the chicken breast topped with barbeque sauce and serve on the side.

5. This salad is a perfect perk-me-up and can be consumed hot or cold.

PART III: DINNER

PORTOBELLO MUSHROOMS WITH MEDITERRANEAN STUFFING

Calorie Content per Serving: Approximately 432.5 – 557.5

Including mushrooms in your dinner is a great choice, as they offer a variety of options to consider. We have included them in this list to provide you with a diverse range of dinner choices.

Ingredients:

- 4 (4-inch) portobello caps (about 3/4 pound)

- 1/4 cup finely chopped onion

- 1/4 cup finely chopped celery

- 1/4 cup finely chopped carrot

- 1/4 cup finely chopped red bell pepper

- 1/4 cup finely chopped green bell pepper

- 1/4 teaspoon dried Italian seasoning

- 2 minced garlic cloves

- cooking spray

- 3 cups (1/4-inch) cubed toasted French bread, toasted

- 1/2 cup vegetable broth

- 1/2 cup (2 ounces) crumbled feta cheese

- 3 tablespoons low-fat balsamic vinaigrette

- 4 teaspoons grated fresh Parmesan cheese

- 1/4 teaspoon black pepper

- 4 cups mixed salad greens

How you make it:

1. Firstly, before starting anything else you must preheat the oven to 350°.

2. Eradicate the stems from the mushrooms and finely chop the stems to measure 1/4 cup. You can discard or keep the remaining stems and use them for some other purpose, depending on you.

3. Combine 1/4 cup chopped stems, onion, celery, carrot, red bell pepper, green bell pepper and Italian seasoning.

4. Heat a large nonstick skillet over medium heat and before eating; coat the pan with cooking spray.

5. Add the onion mixture to the pan and cook for 10 minutes or at least until vegetables are tender enough.

6. Combine the onion mixture and bread in a large bowl and toss it to combine.

7. Slowly add the broth to the bread mixture and toss it to coat properly.

8. Add feta and toss gently. Remove brown gills from the undersides of mushroom caps using a spoon and then discard the gills later on.

9. Place mushrooms in such a way that the stem side should be up. Place them on a baking sheet which is coated with the cooking spray.

10. Brush the mushrooms evenly with 1 tablespoon of vinaigrette.

11. Sprinkle Parmesan and black pepper evenly over the mushrooms and then top each with 1/2 cup bread mixture. |69

12. Bake the mushrooms for 25 minutes at 350 degrees or at least until the mushrooms are tender.

13. Combine the remaining 2 tablespoons of vinaigrette and greens while tossing them gently.

14. Place 1 cup of greens that you have kept for garnishing, on the plate and top the serving with 1 mushroom.

STUFFED TOMATOES

Calorie Content per Serving: Approximately 150–250 calories

Ingredients:

- 2 large tomatoes

- 1/2 cup packaged garlic croutons

- 1/4 cup (1 ounce) crumbled goat cheese

- 1/4 cup sliced pitted kalamata olives

- 2 tablespoons reduced-fat vinaigrette or Italian salad dressing

- 2 tablespoons chopped fresh thyme or basil

How you make it:

1. Firstly preheat the broiler and then cut the tomatoes in half crosswise.

2. Use your finger to push out and discard the seeds. Make sure you use a paring knife to cut out the pulp. You should leave two shells.

3. Then chop the pulp and transfer it to a medium bowl.

4. Place the hollowed tomatoes and cut the sides down on a paper towel. Drain for 5 minutes.

5. Add croutons, goat cheese, olives, dressing, and thyme or basil to pulp and mix them well. Put the mixture into the hollowed tomatoes.

6. Place those tomatoes on a baking sheet or a broiler pan. Broil 4-5 inches from heat until hot and the cheese melts for approximately 5 minutes and then in order to get the best taste just serve immediately.

CHICKEN – GARBANZO SALAD

Ingredients:

- 1 (9-ounce) package of frozen cooked chopped chicken breast

- 1 (15-ounce) rinsed and drained can of chickpeas (garbanzo beans)

- 1 cup chopped seeded cucumber (about 1 small)

- 1/2 cup chopped green onions (about 4 small)

- 1/4 cup chopped fresh mint or basil

- 1/2 cup plain fat-free yogurt

- 2 minced garlic cloves

- 1/4 teaspoon salt

- 2 cups prepackaged baby spinach leaves

- 1/3 cup (1.3 ounces) feta cheese with cracked pepper

- 4 lemon wedges

How you make it:

1. All you have to do is- combine the first 8 ingredients and toss them gently.

2. Gently fold in spinach leaves and feta cheese.

3. Serve the salad with lemon wedges. So easy to make and even easier to serve!

CHICKEN AND TOMATO OMELETS

Calorie Content per Serving: Approximately 450–500 calories

Preparation Time: 30 Minutes

Serves: 4

Ingredients:

- 500 gm Broccoli

- 1.5 cup-sun dried Tomatoes - finely chopped

- 1.5 cups Egg whites

- 2/3 cup low-fat milk

- 2/3 cup Cottage Cheese – low fat

- 3 tbsp. Olive Oil

- 4 – 5 tbsp. Pesto (any store bought recipe will do)

- Salt and Pepper

- 5 oz. roasted/grilled/boiled Chicken breast

- 4 cloves Garlic – finely minced

- 4 tsp Capers

- 4 Oranges

Method:

1. Cover a medium skillet with cooking oil spray, and add the broccoli to it. Add about 2/3 cup water to it and cover.

2. Cook the broccoli for about 5 – 8 minutes, remove from the heat and drain thoroughly.

3. In a large bowl, mix together the egg whites, cottage cheese, pesto, salt, pepper and olive oil, whisking briskly.

4. Add chicken, garlic and capers sun dried tomatoes to this and pour the mixture gently into a clean skillet.

5. Cover and let this cook on medium heat till one side is set. Carefully turn this over, and allow the eggs to finish cooking.

6. Serve hot with slices of oranges for a hearty breakfast meal!

TWO – BEAN GREEK SALAD

Calorie Content per Serving: Approximately 500 calories

Ingredients:

- 2 tablespoons vinegar "of your choice"

- 2 teaspoons Dijon mustard

- 3 teaspoons chopped fresh oregano

- 4 1/2 teaspoons olive oil

- 1/2 teaspoon freshly ground black pepper

- 1 (10-ounce) bag of shelled frozen edamame or lima beans

- 3/4 pound string beans

- 1 cup halved grape tomatoes

- 1/4 cup pitted kalamata olives, halved

- 2 multigrain pitas, halved horizontally

- 3 ounces halloumi cheese (or ricotta salata), sliced into 4 pieces

How you make it:

1. In a serving bowl, whisk together the vinegar, Dijon mustard, 2 1/2 teaspoons oregano, 2 teaspoons olive oil, and 1/4 teaspoon pepper and set them aside.

2. Place the steamer basket in a saucepan filled with a few inches of water and cook edamame which needs to stay covered until it gets tender which is going to be approximately 3 minutes. Transfer this edamame to a bowl and add string beans to the steamer.

3. Cook them properly and again keep them covered until they become tender which means approximately 2 minutes.

4. Now is the time to add beans to edamame. Add tomatoes and olives also and again toss to mix them.

5. Now that you are done with the initial steps, heat a lightly oiled grill pan over a medium-high flame and brush 1 teaspoon oil on one side of the pitas; grill it and keep turning until it turns golden. This is going to take approximately 2 minutes.

6. Transfer pitas to a plate. Again brush 1/2 teaspoon oil evenly on one side of the cheese slices and sprinkle it with the remaining oregano and pepper.

7. Grill cheese in such a way that the seasoned side is facing down.

8. Keep on doing that until marks form which means almost a minute and transfer it to a plate.

9. Place 1 pita and top it with bean salad and cheese. Drizzle with remaining olive oil.

TASTY CABBAGE KIMCHI

As with sauerkraut, you will need a large jar or fermenting crock to make kimchi. This recipe will require two (preferably large) mixing bowls, one large and the other smaller.

Ingredients:

- 1 large Napa cabbage, preferably organic

- 2 tablespoons sea salt

- 2–3 green onions or scallions

- 1 clove garlic, minced or crushed

- 2/3 cup hot red pepper powder

- 1/2 tablespoon stevia

- 2 tablespoons liquid culture, such as yogurt whey, sauerkraut or natural pickle juice, or water kefir

How you make it:

1. Take the outer layer of leaves off the Napa cabbage and discard. Wash the remaining cabbage well.

2. Chop the leaves. Their size should be similar to chopped lettuce in a typical salad.

3. Place the chopped cabbage in the large bowl. Sprinkle in a little sea salt, rub it into the leaves, and mix together.

4. In the smaller bowl, mix the crushed garlic, red pepper powder, stevia, remaining salt, and optional culture. This should form a pasta sauce.

5. Add a spoonful or two of non-chlorinated water if it seems too dry.

6. Pour the sauce paste over the chopped cabbage. Add the chopped green onion. Toss gently until it is coated.

7. Put the kimchi mixture in a glass jar or crock. Cover it loosely with the lid or a cloth. Once the kimchi begins to give off a fermenting smell, probably in 2–3 days, then taste it.

8. As soon as you believe it is ready, you can cover the container and move it to the refrigerator. The fermentation generally takes 3–10 days.

9. Your kimchi will continue to ferment slowly in the refrigerator, where it will last for weeks or months (depending on how sour you can handle it!).

STUFFED ROASTED RED PEPPERS

Ingredients:

- 6 large red bell peppers

- 1 tablespoon olive oil

- 4 minced garlic cloves

- 6 ounces of fresh spinach

- 1 tablespoon fresh lemon juice

- 1 teaspoon salt

- 3/4 cup uncooked couscous (about 2 cups cooked)

- 1/2 cup crumbled feta cheese

How you make it:

The directions are really simple. All you have to do is just take the seeds out of the peppers and stuff them with the mixture formed by the combination of the above-mentioned ingredients and then roast them.

BASMATI SALAD

Ingredients:

- 2 sun-dried tomatoes, packed without oil

- 1/4 cup hot water

- 1 1/4 cups uncooked basmati rice

- 2 cups water

- 1/2 teaspoon salt

- 2/3 cup (2.5 ounces) feta cheese, crumbled

- 2 tablespoons dried currants

- 2 tablespoons chopped fresh mint

- 1 tablespoon olive oil

- 1/4 teaspoon black pepper

- 2 tablespoons toasted pine nuts

How you make it:

1. Combine tomatoes and water in a small bowl and let it stand for 10 minutes.

2. Drain and chop and then set aside. Place the rice in a large bowl and cover with water to 2 inches above the rice.

3. Soak for 30 minutes while stirring occasionally. Now again drain and rinse.

4. Combine the rice and 2 cups of water in a small saucepan and then slowly stir in some salt.

5. Bring to a boil over medium-high flame while stirring frequently. Boil for 5 minutes or until the water level falls just below the level of the rice.

6. Cover it and then reduce the heat to low and cook for 10 minutes. Remove from heat and let it stand, again covered for 10 minutes.

7. Spoon the rice into a bowl and let them cool completely and then fluff them with a fork.

8. After you are done doing this, stir in some tomatoes, feta, and the next 4 ingredients and toss them well to combine.

9. Sprinkle with pine nuts.

MEDITERRANEAN PASTA SALAD

The Mediterranean Pasta Salad is a great option with a calorie content of only 420 per serving and minimal unsaturated fats.

Ingredients:

- 8 ounces multigrain farfalle

- Zest and juice of 1 lemon

- 2 teaspoons olive oil

- 1 13.5- ounce can of artichoke hearts packed in water, drained and chopped

- 8 ounces fresh part- chopped skim mozzarella cheese

- 1/4 cup chopped bottled roasted red bell pepper

- 1/4 cup chopped fresh parsley

- 1/2 cup frozen peas

How you make it:

1. While cooking pasta, make sure you follow the instructions that are provided on the package.

2. Don't forget to get rid of the salt and fat. While your pasta is on the stove, combine the juice of 1 lemon and two teaspoons of olive oil in a large bowl.

3. Make sure you stir it well with a whisk. Now add bell pepper, cheese, artichoke hearts and parsley and toss it to mix well.

4. The next step is to place peas in a colander and right after the pasta is cooked drain the pasta over the peas. Shake them well to drain properly but do not run under cold water at al. now the job is almost done and all you have to do is; add pasta and peas to the artichoke mixture and toss well until the mixture is thoroughly combined. Serve warm or at room temperature depending upon your liking.

PEANUT AND CHICKEN SOUP

Preparation Time: 30 Minutes

Serves: 4

Ingredients:

- 1 medium Onion – chopped

- 2 medium Carrots – chopped

- 1 Bell Pepper – chopped

- 3 large cloves of Garlic – chopped and pressed

- 2 small Jalapeno pepper – finely chopped

- 1 medium Chicken Breast – ground or chopped small

- 2 cups Black Beans

- 3 tins of Chicken Vegetable soup

- 2/3 cup Salsa (any preferred heat) Pinch of Cumin

- 2 large tbsp. smooth Peanut Butter

- 4 – 6 tbsp. cold pressed extra virgin Olive oil

How you make it:

1. In a large Dutch oven, coat the inner walls with cooking spray and place the vessel on a medium high flame till it becomes hot.

2. Add the carrots, onions, garlic and jalapenos and sauté for about 5 minutes.

3. To this, add the chicken and black beans and stir the pot for a few minutes.

4. Now add the soup, salsa and season with the cumin powder. Bring the pot to a boil.

5. Once it boils, reduce the heat to low, and simmer for about 10 minutes.

6. Add the peanut butter and whisk till consistent and allow it to cook for a further 2 minutes.

7. Serve in soup bowls and drizzle the olive oil before consuming hot!

CREAMY ASPARAGUS CHICKEN SOUP WITH SALAD

Calorie Content per Serving: Approximately 362.5–492.5 calories

Preparation Time: 30 minutes

Serves: 2

Ingredients:

- 1 large Onion – finely chopped

- 3 large tbsp. Yogurt – low fat

- 1 cup Chicken Stock

- 1 large Chicken Breast – cut into cubes Cooking spray

- 1 can Asparagus

- 1 cup Onion – chopped finely

- 2 tbsp. cold pressed Olive Oil

- 1 medium pack of Salad leaves with Dressing

- Salt and Pepper – as desired Cooking Spray

How you make it:

1. Lightly spray a medium saucepan with oil and sauté the onions until they become soft and transparent.

2. Add the asparagus and let it cook for a few minutes, and set this mixture aside to cool.

3. Coat the chicken with olive oil lightly and cook in a skillet until light brown.

4. Now add the onions and asparagus to a food processor and blitz with yogurt and chicken stock until almost smooth.

5. Add this to the chicken cooking in the pan and allow it to simmer for about 5 minutes. Stir occasionally and let it simmer without allowing it to come to a boil.

6. Remove when the soup has achieved its desired consistency.

7. Prepare the salad and serve as a side to your delicious soup!

CRANBERRY-ORANGE RELISH

Calorie Content per Serving: Approximately 248 + (calories from yogurt whey or water kefir)

Ingredients:

3 cups fresh cranberries

1/2 cup chopped orange

1/4 cup stevia

1 teaspoon sea salt

1/2 cup orange juice (freshly squeezed is best)

1/2 cup yogurt whey or water kefir Optional: a dash of cinnamon, a little lemon juice

How you make it:

1. Place all ingredients in a food processor and "pulse" it until pieces are finely chopped, but not yet puréed.

2. Transfer relish into a jar, stone crock, or bowl.

3. Cover with a cloth and let it sit for 2–3 days or until the taste is right for you (if you plan to serve it to fermentation newbies, then do not let it get too sour).

4. If needed, add a little more stevia to sweeten it up before eating.

CHICKPEA PATTIES

The good thing about chickpea patties is that they are very easy to make because the total time period of preparing as well as cooking is 20 minutes in total. They have very less number of calories in them; only 225 calories per serving.

Ingredients:

- 1 (15.5-ounce) can of chickpeas, rinsed and drained

- 1/2 cup fresh flat-leaf parsley

- 1 chopped garlic clove

- 1/4 teaspoon ground cumin

- 1/2 teaspoon divided kosher salt

- 1/2 teaspoon divided black pepper

- 1 whisked egg

- 4 tablespoons all-purpose flour

- 2 tablespoons olive oil

- 1/2 cup low-fat Greek-style yogurt

- 3 tablespoons fresh lemon juice

- 8 cups mixed salad greens

- 1 cup grape tomatoes, halved

- 1/2 small thinly sliced red onion

- Pita chips (optional)

How you make It:

1. Pulse chickpeas, flat-leaf parsley, garlic clove, and cumin along with ¼ teaspoon of salt and pepper both, in a food processor, until a viscous chopped mixture comes out now transfer this mixture to a bowl.

2. Now add an egg and two tablespoons of flour to the already prepared mixture.

3. Make around 8 roll patties out of this mixture. Each patty should be approximately ½ inch thick.

4. Do not waste the remaining flour. Put it in a small dish and roll the patties in it with the floured hands. To give it a neat look, tap off the excess flour.

5. Now that you are done with the preparatory phase of the recipe, next up is the cooking phase.

6. First of all, heat the oil in a non-stick skillet over a medium-high flame. Cook the patties from each side for an approximate amount of 2-3 minutes, until they turn a little golden in color.

7. Now whisk some lemon juice and yogurt together and add the remaining salt and pepper to it.

8. Put the garnishing stuff beautifully on the plate which should include green lettuce and tomatoes and onions.

9. You can add other things also, depending upon your own choice. Sprinkle the salad with 2 tablespoons of the dressing.

10. Serve with pita chips if you feel like it.

TOFU ON CURRIED SPINACH

Preparation Time: 30 Minutes

Serves: 1-2

Ingredients:

2 small bags of Spinach – Fresh or Frozen

2 tbsp. Olive Oil

1 tsp Cumin – whole seeds

3 tbsp. Soy Sauce

1 inch Ginger root – peeled and minced

300 gm firm Tofu – roughly cut

1 cup Cream Cheese – low fat

2/3 cup Cilantro – chopped

1 tsp Curry powder

How you make it:

1. Wash the spinach until clean and cut into medium pieces. Wilt the spinach in a small vessel and keep it aside.

2. Heat the olive oil on a skillet and add the cumin and allow SERVE Splutter

3. Add the soy sauce, ginger, chilies, and tofu. Season with salt and pepper.

4. Sauté this over a high flame for about 5 minutes.

5. Lower the heat and add the curry powder. Sauté and add the spinach, and cream cheese while gently stirring.

6. Remove from the heat and garnish with the chopped cilantro.

SEAFOOD SURPRISE SOUP

Preparation Time: 35 minutes

Serves: 1-2

Ingredients:

- 1 small Fennel bulb – chopped and quartered.

- 2 medium leeks – cut into ¼" cubes

- 1/2 Dry Sherry

- 1/2 tsp crushed Pepper

- 1 pinch Salt

- 1 medium Fish Fillet – halibut or any other firm white fish, cubed

- 1/2 pound fresh Mussels – cleaned

- 1 bunch – Flat Leaf Parsley, roughly chopped

- 2/3 cup Mixed Olives

- 1 can Diced/Chopped Tomatoes

- 1 small bag of Salad Leaves

How you make it:

1. Over a medium high heat, heat the oil in a medium saucepan. To this add the leeks, fennel, and garlic and cook for about 3 – 4 minutes, stirring constantly until it is just soft.

2. To this pan, add the tomatoes and the juices and cook for a minute and then add the sherry. Add the salt and bring it to a boil.

3. Now reduce the heat to low and allow it to simmer for about 15 minutes before adding the fish and mussels.

4. Gently stir the pot as it simmers until the fish is cooked, and the mussels have opened. Add the parsley and stir for a minute before removing from the heat.

5. In a large bowl, toss the salad with any preferred dressing and add the olives.

6. Serve the soup hot with the salad on the side.

KEFIR SOUP

Calorie Content per Serving: Approximately 362.5–480 calories

Makes about 4–6 cups

Ingredients:

- 3–3 ½ cups kefir

- 1 large English cucumber, finely chopped or grated

- 1 bunch small radishes, cut in half and thinly sliced (or substitute 1–2 large carrots)

- 1/4 cup chives, finely chopped (you can substitute scallions if you prefer)

- 1/4 cup fresh dill, finely chopped

- 3 hard-boiled eggs, finely chopped

- 1 large beet, boiled or raw, grated

- Salt and pepper to taste

- Water, as needed to thin soup

Optional: Substitute 1 medium potato (steamed or boiled) for beet

Optional: Baby spinach (¼–½ cup), finely chopped

How you Make it:

1. Combine 3 cups of kefir with other ingredients and stir.

2. Add additional kefir or water as needed to thin the soup to desired consistency.

3. Season to taste with salt and pepper.

4. Serve with warm rye bread.

FRESH FRUITY CHICKEN SALAD

Calorie Content per Serving: Approximately 437.5 – 542.5 calories

Preparation Time: 20 Minutes

Serves: 1 – 2

Ingredients:

- 2 medium Chicken Breasts (cooked and chopped into cubes)

- 1 large bag Romaine Lettuce

- 2 medium Salad Tomatoes

- 2 Oz. fresh Grapes (halved)
-
- 1 large Apple (chopped)

- 1 tbsp. cold-pressed Olive Oil

- 1 tbsp. Dijon Mustard

- 3 tsp Light Mayonnaise

- 2 tsp Apple Cider Vinegar

- 1 fresh Lime (squeezed)

- 2 tsp Almonds (thinly sliced)

- 2 tsp Yogurt (low fat)

How you make it:

1. In a salad bowl, toss together the lettuce, apples, grapes and tomatoes with the chicken cubes.

2. In a medium bowl, mix the olive oil, mayonnaise, mustard, vinegar and lime juice to make the salad dressing.

3. Drizzle the salad dressing on the lettuce and toss to spread evenly.

4. Garnish with the almonds and serve!

PART IV: FISH AND SEAFOOD DELIGHTS

GRILLED SALMON WITH LEMON HERB SAUCE

Calorie Content per Serving: Approximately 250 calories

Preparation Time: 25 minutes

SERVES: 4

Ingredients:

- Salmon fillets (4, skin-on)

- Olive oil (2 tablespoons)

- Lemon juice (2 tablespoons)

- Fresh herbs (such as dill, parsley, or basil) (2 tablespoons, chopped)

- Garlic (2 cloves, minced)

- Salt (to taste)

- Black pepper (to taste)

How to make it:

1. Preheat the grill to medium-high heat.

2. In a small bowl, mix together olive oil, lemon juice, minced garlic, and chopped fresh herbs.

3. Season the salmon fillets with salt and black pepper on both sides.

4. Brush the salmon fillets with the prepared lemon herb sauce.

5. Place the salmon fillets on the preheated grill, skin side down.

6. Grill for about 4-6 minutes per side, depending on the thickness of the fillets, until the salmon is cooked through and flakes easily with a fork.

7. Remove the grilled salmon from the grill and let it rest for a few minutes.

8. Serve the grilled salmon with additional lemon wedges and garnish with fresh herbs. Enjoy!

SHRIMP SCAMPI WITH ZUCCHINI NOODLES

Calorie Content per Serving: Approximately 388–430 calories

Preparation Time: 20 minutes

SERVES: 4

Ingredients:

- Shrimp (1 pound, peeled and deveined)

- Zucchini (4 medium, spiralized into noodles)

- Olive oil (2 tablespoons)

- Garlic (4 cloves, minced)

- Red pepper flakes (1/4 teaspoon, optional)

- Lemon juice (2 tablespoons)

- Salt (to taste)

- Black pepper (to taste)

- Fresh parsley (2 tablespoons, chopped)

How to make it:

1. Heat olive oil in a large skillet over medium heat.

2. Add minced garlic and red pepper flakes (if using) to the skillet and sauté for about 1 minute until fragrant.

3. Add the shrimp to the skillet and cook for 2-3 minutes per side until they turn pink and opaque.

4. Remove the cooked shrimp from the skillet and set aside.

5. In the same skillet, add the zucchini noodles and sauté for about 2-3 minutes until slightly softened but still crisp.

6. Return the cooked shrimp to the skillet with the zucchini noodles.

7. Drizzle lemon juice over the shrimp and zucchini noodles.

8. Season with salt and black pepper to taste.

9. Toss everything together gently until well combined and heated through.

10. Remove from heat and sprinkle with fresh chopped parsley.

11. Serve the shrimp scampi with zucchini noodles hot. Enjoy!

PAN–SEARED HALIBUT WITH MANGO SALSA

Calorie Content per Serving: Approximately 254–258 calories

Calorie Content per Serving: Manga Salsa: Approximately 189–200 calories

Preparation Time: 30 minutes

SERVES: 4

Ingredients:

- Halibut fillets (4, skinless)

- Olive oil (2 tablespoons)

- Lime juice (2 tablespoons)

- Garlic powder (1 teaspoon)

- Paprika (1 teaspoon)

- Salt (to taste)

- Black pepper (to taste)

Mango Salsa:

- Mango (1 large, diced)

- Red bell pepper (1/2, diced)

- Red onion (1/4 cup, finely chopped)

- Fresh cilantro (2 tablespoons, chopped)

- Lime juice (1 tablespoon)

- Salt (to taste)

- Black pepper (to taste)

How to make it:

1. In a small bowl, mix together olive oil, lime juice, garlic powder, paprika, salt, and black pepper.

2. Pat the halibut fillets dry with a paper towel and brush both sides with the prepared marinade.

3. Heat a non-stick skillet over medium-high heat.

4. Add the halibut fillets to the skillet and cook for about 3-4 minutes per side until golden brown and cooked through.

5. Meanwhile, in a separate bowl, combine diced mango, diced red bell pepper, finely chopped red onion, chopped cilantro, lime juice, salt, and black pepper to make the mango salsa.

6. Remove the cooked halibut fillets from the skillet and let them rest for a few minutes.

7. Serve the pan-seared halibut with a generous spoonful of mango salsa on top. Enjoy!

LEMON GARLIC BUTTER COD

Calorie Content per Serving: Approximately 414–518 calories

Preparation Time: 25 minutes

SERVES: 4

Ingredients:

- Cod fillets (4, skinless)

- Butter (4 tablespoons)

- Lemon juice (2 tablespoons)

- Garlic (4 cloves, minced)

- Fresh parsley (2 tablespoons, chopped)

- Salt (to taste)

- Black pepper (to taste)

How to make it:

1. Preheat the oven to 400°F (200°C).

2. In a small saucepan, melt the butter over low heat.

3. Add minced garlic, lemon juice, chopped fresh parsley, salt, and black pepper to the melted butter. Stir well to combine.

4. Place the cod fillets in a baking dish and pour the lemon garlic butter sauce over them.

5. Bake the cod fillets in the preheated oven for about 12-15 minutes until the fish is opaque and flakes easily with a fork.

6. Remove from the oven and let the cod fillets rest for a few minutes.

7. Serve the lemon garlic butter cod hot with additional fresh parsley for garnish. Enjoy!

GARLIC BUTTER SHRIMP STIR–FRY

Preparation Time: 20 minutes

Serves: 4

Ingredients:

- Shrimp (1 pound, peeled and deveined)

- Butter (4 tablespoons)

- Garlic (4 cloves, minced)

- Red bell pepper (1, sliced)

- Sugar snap peas (1 cup)

- Carrot (1, julienned)

- Soy sauce (2 tablespoons, low-sodium)

- Sesame oil (1 tablespoon)

- Salt (to taste)

- Black pepper (to taste)

- Sesame seeds (for garnish)

How to make it:

1. In a large skillet or wok, melt the butter over medium heat.

2. Add minced garlic to the skillet and sauté for about 1 minute until fragrant.

3. Add sliced red bell pepper, sugar snap peas, and julienned carrot to the skillet. Stir-fry for about 4-5 minutes until the vegetables are crisp-tender.

4. Push the vegetables to one side of the skillet and add the shrimp to the other side.

5. Cook the shrimp for about 2-3 minutes per side until they turn pink and opaque.

6. Stir in soy sauce and sesame oil. Season with salt and black pepper to taste.

7. Toss everything together until well combined and heated through.

8. Remove from heat and sprinkle with sesame seeds for garnish.

9. Serve the garlic butter shrimp stir-fry hot over steamed rice or noodles. Enjoy!

10. Aim to make fermented meat, fish and eggs a part of your daily diet.

BAKED DIJON SALMON

Calorie Content per Serving: Approximately 126–168 calories

Preparation Time: 30 minutes

SERVES: 4

Ingredients:

- Salmon fillets (4, skin-on)

- Dijon mustard (2 tablespoons)

- Honey (1 tablespoon)

- Garlic (2 cloves, minced)

- Fresh dill (2 tablespoons, chopped)

- Salt (to taste)

- Black pepper (to taste)

- Lemon wedges (for serving)

How to make it:

1. Preheat the oven to 400°F (200°C).

2. In a small bowl, whisk together Dijon mustard, honey, minced garlic, chopped fresh dill, salt, and black pepper.

3. Place the salmon fillets in a baking dish, skin side down.

4. Brush the Dijon mustard mixture evenly over the top of each salmon fillet.

5. Bake the salmon in the preheated oven for about 12-15 minutes until the fish is cooked through and flakes easily with a fork.

6. Remove from the oven and let the salmon rest for a few minutes.

7. Serve the baked Dijon salmon hot with lemon wedges on the side. Enjoy!

SEARED TUNA STEAK WITH AVOCADO SALSA

Preparation Time: 20 minutes

SERVES: 4

Ingredients:

- Tuna steaks (4, about 6 ounces each)

- Olive oil (2 tablespoons)

- Lime juice (2 tablespoons)

- Salt (to taste)

- Black pepper (to taste)

Avocado Salsa:

- Avocado (1 large, diced)

- Tomato (1 large, diced)

- Red onion (1/4 cup, finely chopped)

- Jalapeño (1, seeded and minced)

- Fresh cilantro (2 tablespoons, chopped)

- Lime juice (1 tablespoon)

- Salt (to taste)

- Black pepper (to taste)

How to make it:

1. In a shallow dish, combine olive oil, lime juice, salt, and black pepper.

2. Place the tuna steaks in the marinade and turn to coat both sides. Let them marinate for about 10 minutes.

3. Meanwhile, in a separate bowl, combine diced avocado, diced tomato, finely chopped red onion, minced jalapeño, chopped cilantro, lime juice, salt, and black pepper to make the avocado salsa.

4. Heat a non-stick skillet or grill pan over high heat.

5. Remove the tuna steaks from the marinade and pat them dry with a paper towel.

6. Sear the tuna steaks for about 1-2 minutes per side until they are browned on the outside but still pink in the center.

7. Remove the seared tuna steaks from the skillet and let them rest for a few minutes.

8. Serve the tuna steaks with a generous spoonful of avocado salsa on top. Enjoy!

SPICY GRILLED SHRIMP SKEWERS

Calorie Content per Serving: Approximately 368–400 calories

Preparation Time: 30 minutes

Serves: 4

Ingredients:

- Shrimp (1 pound, peeled and deveined)

- Olive oil (2 tablespoons)

- Lime juice (2 tablespoons)

- Garlic (2 cloves, minced)

- Smoked paprika (1 teaspoon)

- Cayenne pepper (1/2 teaspoon, or to taste)

- Salt (to taste)

- Black pepper (to taste)

- Wooden skewers (soaked in water for 30 minutes)

How to make it:

1. In a small bowl, whisk together olive oil, lime juice, minced garlic, smoked paprika, cayenne pepper, salt, and black pepper.

2. Place the shrimp in a shallow dish and pour the marinade over them. Toss to coat the shrimp evenly.

3. Cover the dish and let the shrimp marinate in the refrigerator for about 15-20 minutes.

4. Preheat the grill to medium-high heat.

5. Thread the marinated shrimp onto the soaked wooden skewers.

6. Grill the shrimp skewers for about 2-3 minutes per side until they are pink and opaque.

7. Remove the grilled shrimp skewers from the grill and let them rest for a few minutes.

8. Serve the spicy grilled shrimp skewers hot as an appetizer or main dish. Enjoy!

PART V: DESSERTS

CREAMY RICE PUDDING WITH BLUEBERRY COMPOTE

Calorie Content per Serving: Approximately 174.3–281.25 calories

Preparation Time: 1 Hour

Serves: 8 – 10

Ingredients:

- 1 ½ cups Basmati Rice – brown, organic

- 2 ½ cups Water

- 1 pinch Salt

- 4 cups Rice Milk

- 1/2 cup Stevia

- 2 tbsp. Potato Starch Cinnamon powder – to taste For the Blueberry Compote:

- 3 cups fresh, organic Blueberries

- 1/2 cup brown Sugar/ Stevia

- 1/4 cup Water

How you make it:

1. Add the rice and water to a medium saucepan and bring to a boil. Add the salt and gently stir the contents.

2. Once boiled, reduce the heat to a low, and simmer the rice. Fold the rice in gently until all the water is fully absorbed.

3. Add to this, the brown sugar/ Stevia and 2 pinches of cinnamon powder and mix. Add the rice milk and continue to cook for about 10 minutes.

4. Dissolve the potato starch in a few tablespoons of water and add to the rice mix.

5. Allow the mixture to simmer on low heat until it thickens and remove it from the heat.

6. Allow to cool, and transfer to a bowl. Place the bowl in the fridge and allow it to cool.

7. In a small saucepan on medium heat, crush the blueberries to a small pot and add the sugar and water.

8. Bring to a boil and allow it to simmer. Remove from the heat after a minute or two.

9. Once chilled, serve with the warm Blueberry compote.

GARLIC KALE HUMMUS

Calorie Content per Serving: Approximately 135–195 calories

Serves: 4

Ingredients:

- 2 cups Cooked Chickpeas

- 1 cup Torn and Washed Kale

- 1/2 teaspoon Fresh Chopped Garlic

- 1/2 teaspoon Onion Powder

- 1/4 teaspoon Black Pepper

- 1/4 cup Water

How you make it:

1. Combine chickpeas, Kale, Spices, and Water in a blender or food processor and then blend it until it becomes a smooth mixture.

2. Let it chill in the fridge and store it in an airtight container for about 1 week.

SAVOURY SWEET CARROT MUFFINS

Calorie Content: Serves–10: Approximately 243–316 calories

Preparation Time: 30 Minutes

Serves: 10 – 12

Ingredients:

- 1 ½ cup Milk/Rice Milk

- 2 small Eggs

- 4-5 tbsp. Canola Oil

- 3 cups Quinoa/Gluten-free flour

- 4 tbsp. Stevia

- 2 tbsp. Flaxseed meal

- 2 tsp Baking Powder (gluten-free)

- 1 pinch Salt

- 1 pinch Cinnamon powder

- 3 medium Organic Carrots (grated)

- ½ cup Raisins

How you make it:

1. Preheat an oven to about 400oF. In a bowl, whisk the egg with the oil and milk.

2. In another bowl, mix the dry ingredients, and add them to the wet mix, stirring gently till well blended.

3. Add the grated carrots and the raisins to the batter and fold the mixture.

4. In a muffin pan, grease the muffin molds or line them with muffin cups. Fill the cups till about 2/3 full.

5. Bake this in the oven for about 20 minutes. Remove from the oven and place on a wire rack to cool. Enjoy!

TOASTED BREAD WITH CHOCOLATE

Calorie Content per Serving: Approximately 255–340 calories

Serves: 4

Ingredients:

- 8 1/2-inch-thick slices of good bread

- Best-quality extra-virgin olive oil for drizzling

- 4 oz. best-quality bittersweet chocolate, very coarsely chopped (scant 1 cup)

- Sea salt

- kosher salt or any specialty salt

How you make it:

1. Position a rack 4 inches from the broiler element and heat it to a high temperature.

2. Put the bread on a baking sheet and toast until it becomes light golden on both sides. This will take 1 to 2 minutes per side.

3. Drizzle the bread with olive oil. Distribute the chocolate evenly on top of the bread.

4. Turn off the broiler and return the bread to the oven until the residual heat melts the chocolate.

5. This should not take more than 1 minute. Smooth the chocolate with a table knife, if you want.

6. Sprinkle a pinch of salt on each slice and serve.

FRESH MILLET PANCAKES WITH FRUIT COMPOTE

Calorie Content: Serves–4: Approximately 376.25–475 calories

Preparation Time: 45 Minutes

Serves: 3 – 4

Ingredients:

- 1 ½ cup Millet grains

- 3 tbsp. ground Millet flour

- 2 cups Skimmed milk

- 1 pinch Salt

- 100 ml of Carbonated Water

- 2 tbsp. Stevia

- ½ cup Yogurt (non-fat, plain)

- 2 Eggs, lightly beaten

- 500 gm dried, pitted organic Plums

- 3 cups Water

- 3 tbsp. Apple juice

How you make it:

1. In a medium saucepan, add the milk, millets, and salt and bring to a boil over medium heat.

2. Once it comes up to a boil, bring the heat down to a simmer and cover for 20 minutes until the milk is absorbed by the millet.

3. Gently mash the millets to a paste, and fold in the yogurt, eggs and sugar with the millet flour. Add the carbonated water to make the batter to your desired consistency.

4. In a separate bowl, add the cherries to warm water and allow it to soften.

5. Preheat a non-stick skillet on medium heat, and spray with vegetable cooking spray. Ladle the batter onto the skillet using a spoon and shape it into a pancake disk.

6. Gently cook each side for about 3-4 minutes until golden brown and flip over to repeat the same for the other side.

7. In another saucepan, add the plums, sugar and water and bring to a boil.

8. Add the apple juice and allow to simmer for about 15 minutes until the plums are soft.

9. Plate the pancakes and serve with the compote.

PROSCIUTTO WITH ARTICHOKE AND ARUGULA PIZZA

Calorie Content: Serves—8: Approximately 2035—285 calories

This recipe thrives on a harmonious blend of flavors. The bitter notes of arugula, the sweetness of artichoke, the saltiness of prosciutto, and the creaminess of mozzarella coexist in perfect balance on a delightful crust accompanied by pesto sauce. Not only does this combination offer a more gratifying experience than the classic pepperoni and red sauce, but it also bakes in a mere 11 minutes, no longer than a frozen pizza. With such an incredible option before you, isn't it truly remarkable?

It is difficult to determine the exact number of servings for this recipe. However, given the size of the pizza (14 x 10-inch rectangle) and the instructions to cut it into 4 (7 x 5-inch) rectangles, it is likely that the recipe would serve approximately 8 people.

Please note that the number of servings may vary depending on personal preferences and portion sizes.

Ingredients:

- Cooking spray

- 1 tablespoon cornmeal

- 1 (13.8-ounce) can of refrigerated pizza crust dough

- 2 tablespoons commercial pesto

- 1/2 cup (2 ounces) shredded part-skim mozzarella cheese

- 1 (9-ounce) package of frozen artichoke hearts, thawed and drained

- 1 ounce thinly sliced prosciutto

- 2 tablespoons shredded Parmesan cheese

- 1 1/2 cups arugula leaves

- 1 1/2 tablespoons fresh lemon juice

How you make it:

1. The first and foremost thing that you need to do is to position the oven rack to the lowest setting. And then like any other baking recipe, you have to preheat the oven to a temperature of 500°.

2. Now, coat a baking sheet with cooking spray and sprinkle it with cornmeal.

3. Unroll the dough onto the prepared baking sheet, and pat it into a 14 x 10-inch rectangle.

4. Now make sure you spread the pesto evenly over the dough, leaving a 1/2-inch border.

5. The next step is to sprinkle mozzarella cheese over the pesto. Place the baking sheet on the bottom oven rack and bake at 500° for a minimum of 5 minutes.

6. After that, remove the pizza from the oven. Coarsely chop the artichokes. Arrange artichokes on pizza and top with sliced prosciutto. Sprinkle with Parmesan.

7. Return the pizza to the bottom oven rack and now bake for an additional 6 minutes or until the crust is browned.

8. Now place the arugula in a bowl and drizzle juice over the arugula and toss gently. Top the pizza with arugula mixture. Cut the pizza into 4 (7 x 5-inch) rectangles and cut each rectangle diagonally into 2 wedges.

PROBIOTIC CANTALOUPE SMOOTHIE

Calorie Content: Serves—2: Approximately 240—290 calories

Preparation Time: 15 Minutes

Serves: 1 - 2

Ingredients:

- Cantaloupe

- Probiotic Yogurt

- Vanilla bean

- Organic Honey

- Crushed Ice

How you make it:

1. Add all the ingredients to a blender and blitz until smooth.

2. Pour into a tall smoothie glass and garnish with a mint leaf and slice of lime.

3. Serve chilled.

CREPE DE QUINOA ET APPLESAUCE

Calorie Content: Serves—10: Approximately 186.5 calories

Preparation Time: 30 Minutes

Serves: 10 – 12

Ingredients:

- 1 ½ cups Organic Quinoa flour

- ½ cup Organic Tapioca flour

- 1 pinch of Baking Soda powder

- 400 ml Sparkling water

- 4 tbsp. Canola oil

- 1 small tsp Cinnamon powder

- 4 cups Organic Applesauce – unsweetened

How you make it:

1. Mix both the flour in a medium bowl with the baking soda. Add the cinnamon powder and mix gently.

2. Stir in the canola oil and carbonated sparkling water to this, until the batter reaches the desired consistency. Check for lumps, and stir till smooth.

3. Place a non-stick skillet on medium heat, add a few drops of oil and spread it to grease the skillet.

4. Pour about 3 tablespoons of the batter and rotate the skillet to spread it to form the crepe.

5. Cook until the side is a light golden brown and flip over gently.

6. Keep making crepes until the batter runs out.

7. Serve the crepes hot with the applesauce.

RASPBERRY APPLE CRUMBLE

Preparation Time: 1 Hour 15 minutes

Serves: 4- 6

Ingredients:

- 6 large cooking Apples – thinly sliced

- 1 cup Raspberries

- 2.5 cups Apple Juice

- 2.5 cups Rolled Oats

- ¼ cup Butter (or) Margarine

- 3 tbsp. Brown Sugar/stevia

- 1.5 tsp Cinnamon powder

- 1.5 tbsp. Clove powder

How you make it:

1. Preheat the oven to 350oF. In a greased baking dish, arrange the sliced apple and raspberries and pour the apple juice to cover this.

2. In a bowl, mix the rolled oats, stevia, or brown sugar and spices to form a rough flour. To this, add the butter and mix in with your fingers to make the crumble topping.

3. Layer the crumble topping onto the laid-out apples and raspberries until they are covered with a uniform layer. Bake for about 45 – 60 minutes.

4. This crumble can be served hot or cold.

BUTTER ALMOND COOKIES

Preparation Time: 30 Minutes

SERVES: 6 – 10

Ingredients:

- 1/2 cup Organic Coconut oil / Organic Butter

- 3/4 cup Organic Coconut Sugar

- 1 Egg

- 1 teaspoon Vanilla Extract (or) 1 whole Vanilla Bean (slit and extract the seeds)

- 1.5 cups Almond Flour

- 1 cup Almond Butter (Crunchy or Smooth)

- 1 pinch of Sea Salt

- 1/2 cup Coconut Flour

How you make it:

1. Preheat the oven to 350oF.

2. In a bowl, add the coconut oil, almond butter and sugar and mix well using a spatula.

3. Add the egg, salt and vanilla and mix together until smooth.

4. To this, add the almond flour and the coconut flour and mix well to form a firm dough.

5. Allow to set for 10 minutes, then use a tablespoon to scoop out a small ball and place it onto a greased cookie tray.

6. You can use a fork to flatten the dough – this also gives the dough a nice design if you press down in a crisscross pattern.

7. Place as many cookie balls as you can and flatten them so that they don't touch each other. The dough does not expand, so there's no worry about loading the tray too full.

8. Place the cookie tray in the oven, and bake for 10-12 minutes at 350o. Remove the tray from the oven and allow the cookies to cool.

9. Use a spatula to gently transfer the cookies onto a cooling rack and enjoy!

POCKET-SIZED BUTTERMINTS

Calorie Content: Serves–6: Approximately 178.16 calories

Preparation Time: 2 hours 10 minutes

SERVES: 6 – 10

Yield: Approximately 60 small-sized Buttermints.

Ingredients:

- ½ cup Butter (Pasteurized) (or) ½ cup Organic Cold Pressed (Virgin) Coconut oil

- 4 Tbsp. Organic Raw Honey

- 10 - 14 drops Peppermint essential oil (or) 5 – 10 drops Peppermint oil

How you make it:

1. Keep the butter at room temperature. In a bowl, add all the ingredients and stir to combine. Add peppermint oil or extract to suit your taste.

2. Add the mixture to a pastry bag, squeeze out button-sized servings onto a parchment-lined baking tray, and place in the fridge for about 2 hours till the mints set.

3. You can then transfer this to a storage container that can be kept in the fridge.

4. For the recipe with coconut oil, mix all the ingredients and pour the batter onto a parchment-lined baking tray.

5. As this batter will be softer than the butter batter, you won't be able to pipe this into button-sized servings.

6. Place this in the fridge for 2 hours; allow setting, and simply cut into squares. Transfer this to the storage container and keep it in the fridge.

STRAWBERRY GELATO

Preparation Time: 5 hours 30 minutes

Serves: 6+

Ingredients:

- 1/4 cup Butter/Coconut oil (or) 1 cup Heavy Cream

- 4 Egg yolks

- 2 cups Milk / Coconut milk (if lactose intolerant)

- 1/2 cup Maple Syrup/Honey/Stevia Tincture

- 2 cups Fresh Strawberries, stemmed with tops removed and pureed

- A pinch of sea salt

- Lemon Zest – optional (Half tsp).

How you make it:

1. In a saucepan, add the milk and cream and bring to a boil. After this, allow the mix to simmer, while constantly stirring for about 4-5 minutes.

2. In a blender, whisk the egg yolk, honey, and salt till you get a smooth and creamy mix. Continue to whisk on a low speed, slowly adding the warm milk mixture.

3. You have to be very careful at this stage or you can end up with cooked eggs.

4. Once the milk has been added, carefully empty the contents into the saucepan over a medium low heat, and stir constantly till the mix starts to thicken.

5. To this, add the pureed strawberries and lemon zest and combine thoroughly.

6. Allow the mixture to chill in a refrigerator for a minimum of 4-5 hours till it is completely cooled down. Leaving it overnight in the fridge will make a deeper, intensive flavor.

7. Once the mixture is completely chilled, add this to an ice cream maker to make the gelato.

8. In case you don't have an ice cream maker, you can make this in the blender/food processor by simply freezing the mixture for 2-3 hours, blitzing it in the blender till smooth, and then refreezing it for another 2-3 hours.

FUDGY SWEET POTATO BROWNIES

Calorie Content: Serves—4: Approximately 436.25 calories

Preparation Time: 40 Minutes

Serves: 4

Ingredients:

- 1/4 cup cold pressed Coconut Oil

- 1/3 cup unsweetened Cocoa Powder

- 1/2 cup Pastry Flour (Whole Wheat preferred)

- 1 pinch Baking Powder

- 1 pinch of fine Sea Salt

- 1 cup Coconut Sugar

- 1 cup Sweet Potato Puree

- 1 Tbsp. ground flaxseed meal + 3 Tbsp. cool water

- 1½ tsp pure vanilla extract

How you make it:

1. In a small bowl, add the flour, salt and baking powder and mix well.

2. Place a saucepan on a low flame and melt the coconut oil. Stir in the cocoa powder until the entire mix is smooth.

3. Add the sweet potato, flax seed meal, water, sugar and vanilla to a large bowl and whisk thoroughly. You might need to keep at it for a bit as the coconut sugar can take a bit of time.

4. Add the cocoa and coconut oil mixture to the large bowl and keep whisking.

5. Add flour to this and keep whisking till smooth and the batter has a glossy appearance.

6. Lightly grease an 8"x8" glass baking pan with coconut oil, and preheat the oven to 350o.

7. Pour the batter into the pan, and bake for 20 to 30 minutes. The top should appear hard and baked. When you stick a butter knife into the center, it should come out smooth with a few moist crumbs.

Note: The total baking time will depend on what type of sweet potatoes you use. In case you use canned puree, it can take a bit longer as they have higher moisture content.

Stir in the flour till smooth, scrap into the prepared pan.

PART VI: BEVERAGES

OUTLIVED TEA

Calorie Content per Serving: Approximately 82 calories (with Honey)

Preparation Time: 5 Minutes

Ingredients:

2 1-inch fresh ginger, sliced

0.5-inch fresh turmeric, sliced

1 tsp. fennel seeds

400ml Water

Optional – Raw Honey

How you make it:

1. Boil the water in a teapot, remove it from the stove, and add the ingredients.

2. Allow this to steep for five minutes.

3. Fennel adds its natural sweetness to this brew, however, you can also add a spoon of raw organic honey – this combo is a winner, especially when you want to reduce inflammation.

ULTIMATE BRAIN SMOOTHIE

Calorie Content: Serve–3 Approximately 296–350 calories (with honey or maple syrup)

Preparation Time: 5 Minutes

Serves: 3

Ingredients:

1 cup Fresh Berries

1 full, compact cup of Leafy greens

1.5 inch (4 cm) piece of ginger

1 tablespoon Cold Pressed Coconut Oil

1 teaspoon fresh Chia seeds

300 ml Green tea

Optional – Honey/Maple Syrup to sweeten

How you make it:

1. Add the ingredients to a blender, and blitz.

2. Add green tea to dilute to your desired consistency.

3. Consume immediately.

NERVE CALMING JUICE

Preparation Time: 5 Minute

Serves: 3

Ingredients:

- 1/3 Pineapple

- 4 sticks of Celery

- 1 head Romaine Lettuce

- 1 small Cucumber

- 1-inch Ginger

- 100 ml Water

How you make it:

1. Add all the ingredients to a blender; add a few cubes of ice and about 100 ml of water.

2. Blend till smooth.

3. Serve cold.

TURMERIC TEA

Preparation Time: 15 minutes

Serves: 2

Ingredients:

- 8 ounces of almond milk

- ½ Tsp Turmeric

- A pinch of Cayenne Pepper Powder

- ½ tsp Honey

- 1/8 cinnamon powder

How you make it:

1. Add milk to a vessel and place over a medium-high flame. Bring the milk to a boil.

2. Add the remaining ingredients and allow this to simmer for 5-7 mins.

3. Serve hot.

CITRUS GREEN TEA

Preparation Time: 10 minutes

SERVES: 2

Ingredients:

- 1 tsp of lemon juice

- 2 cups of water

- 1 teabag of Chinese green tea

- Optional – Honey to sweeten.

How you make it:

1. Boil the two cups of water with the lemon juice.

2. Remove the boiling water and add the tea bag. Allow the bag to steep for about 3-5 minutes.

3. Optionally, you can add honey once you have steeped the tea bag.

DELICIOUS AFRICAN MILLET BEVERAGE

Calorie Content: 2–cups: Approximately 262–344 calories

Makes about 2 cups Koko can be prepared as a drink or a porridge. Traditionally, the raw liquid portion of this is boiled, then cooled, and mixed with the raw, cultured solids to make a fermented gruel or porridge. Feel free to try this as well: I prefer to drink the liquid and feed the solids to the chickens, but perhaps you like spiced millet more than I do! There are many variations of this in West and Central Africa. This is a slightly simplified recipe.

Ingredients:

- 2 cups water

- 1 cup CRASH milk, preferably almond milk

- 1/2 cup millet or sorghum grain

- 1 tablespoon yogurt whey or water kefir

- 1-inch ginger root, peeled and finely chopped

- 1/4 Tsp ground cloves

- 1/4 Tsp cardamom

- 1/4 Tsp cinnamon

- 1/2 Tsp sea salt

- 1/8 Tsp each: cayenne pepper and black

- pepper

- Maple syrup, to taste

How you make it:

1. Soak millet in water for 8–12 hours.

2. Grind or crush in a food processor or by using a mortar and pestle.

3. Add spices and salt. Move to a jar, container, or pot and cover with water.

4. Cover the container and let it ferment at room temperature for 2–3 hours.

5. Pour liquid into a glass, add sweetener to taste, and enjoy.

HIBISCUS TEA

Calorie Content: Serves 6–8: Approximately 145 calories

Preparation Time: 35 minutes

SERVES: 6 to 8

Ingredients:

- Water (48 ounces)

- Hibiscus tea leaf/tea bag (3 tablespoons)

- Cinnamon sticks (2)

- Brown sugar/Stevia (1/8 cup)

- Orange (1 small, sliced)

- Lemon (1, cut into wedges)

How you make it:

1. Bring water to a light boil, and turn off the heat.

2. Add the hibiscus flowers and cinnamon sticks. Cover with a lid and allow the tea to steep for 20 minutes.

3. Strain tea into desired container, add sugar and orange slices and serve over ice. Garnish each glass with a lemon slice.

CINNAMON TEA

Calorie Content per Serving: Serves—2: Approximately 245 calories

Preparation Time: 10 Minutes

SERVES: 2

Ingredients:

- 1 2" cinnamon stick (or) a teaspoon of ground cinnamon

- Boiling water – 500 ml Optional –Loose Tea/ Any favorite flavored Tea Bag

- Honey

- Milk

- 1 Slice – Orange or Lemon

How you make it:

1. To your favorite cup, add one-half of the cinnamon stick, or half a teaspoon of the ground powder.

2. Add about 200ml boiling water.

3. Let your cinnamon tea steep for 8 to 10 minutes.

4. If you're using the cinnamon stick, remove the pieces.

Optional – You can add the teabag or loose tea (in an infuser) with the orange or lemon slice, and allow the tea to steep for another couple of minutes.

PART VII: MY OUTLIVE 7 DAY MEAL PLAN

The 7 Day Meal Plan aims to simplify the Outlived Diet and make it enjoyable, even with a busy schedule. With these straightforward and delightful recipes, your week will be filled with easy-to-make meals that will add a touch of brightness.

Feel free to mix and match the delicious breakfast and main course options for a varied and satisfying experience!

The Outlive 7-day meal plan:

DAY 1

Breakfast: Raspberry Green Tea Power Smoothie

Beverage: Cinnamon Tea

Lunch: BBQ Chicken Salad

Dinner: Chicken Tomato Omelette

Dessert: Probiotic Cantaloupe Smoothie

DAY 2

Breakfast: Sweet Spiced Oats

Beverage: Citrus Green Tea

Lunch: Nourishing Kimchi Noodles

Dinner: Peanut and Chicken Soup

Dessert: Crepe de Quinoa et Applesauce

DAY 3

Breakfast: Oriental Baked Omelets

Beverage: Outlive Tea

Lunch: Broccoli Salad with Baked Chicken

Dinner: Seafood Surprise Soup

Dessert: Raspberry Apple Crumble

DAY 4

Breakfast: Quinoa Buckwheat Flapjacks

Beverage: Ultimate Brain Smoothie

Lunch: Fresh Fruity Chicken Salad

Dinner: Creamy Asparagus Chicken Soup and Salad

Dessert: Butter Almond Cookies

DAY 5

Breakfast: Nutty Protein Oats

Beverage: Nerve Calming Juice

Lunch: Tasty Radish Kimchi

Dinner: Tasty Garbage Kimchi

Dessert: Garlic Kale Hummus

DAY 6

Breakfast: Oriental Baked Omelettes

Beverage: Citrus Green Tea

Lunch: Avocado, Turkey and Black Bean Cheese Salad

Dinner: Delicious Kefir Soup

Dessert: Strawberry Gelato

DAY 7

Breakfast: Baked Cheesy Eggs

Beverage: Hibiscus Tea

Lunch: Pasta Orzo and Tomatoes

Dinner: Chicken and Tomatoes Omelets

Dessert: Fudgy Sweet Potato Brownies

Thank you!

We are constantly striving to provide the ideal experience for the community, and your input helps us to define that experience. So we kindly ask you when you have free time take a minute to post a review on Amazon.

Thank you for helping us support our passions.

TO LEAVE A REVIEW, JUST SCAN THE QR CODE BELOW:

OR YOU CAN GO TO:

amazon.com/review/create-review/

Made in United States
North Haven, CT
03 August 2023